LOOKING AFTER CORPORATE HEALTH

Philip Hayes

PERSONNEL
Today

LOOKING AFTER
CORPORATE HEALTH

John Humphrey and Paul Smith

Pitman Publishing
128 Long Acre, London WC2E 9AN

A Division of Longman Group UK Limited

First published in Great Britain 1991

British Library Cataloguing in Publication Data

Humphrey, John
    Looking after corporate health. — (Personnel
    today)
    I. Title II. Smith, Paul III. Series
    658.3

ISBN 0 273 03719 6

Typeset, printed and bound in Great Britain

Contents

Other books in this series

Making Equal Opportunities Work
Mary Coussey and Hilary Jackson

Taking Care of Safety
Roger Saunders

Acknowledgements

The content of this book draws heavily on the work of others. Their research is referred to in the text, and the sources are presented in the Bibliography. We would particularly like to thank those who have contributed specific information for the book, and those who have read the text and provided invaluable advice. They include Lewis Ritchie, Michael Peel, Lawrence Purchase, Tim Carter and Anne Kennaugh. Many of our observations are based on the work of colleagues, especially Melvyn Percy and Christopher Packard.

Foreword

The health of those at work is rarely the first concern of any manager, yet a healthy workforce is one of the prime resources on which the success of an organisation depends. The costs and disruption caused by illness in key staff can be substantial and sometimes disastrous for the whole future of a company. Health at work can be improved not only by preventing disease caused by work but also by maintaining conditions in the workplace that support a healthy lifestyle, and by health promotion activities directed at reducing the toll taken by diseases such as heart attacks and cancers.

It is both practicable and cost effective for an organisation to improve the health of its staff. The starting point must be an assessment of the likely risks to health backed up by effective intervention to minimise harm. This requires a shared commitment from management and staff alike. The preventive action required will depend on the nature of work activities, the numbers of staff and their distribution. Competent advice is needed to ensure that actions are targeted to important problems and that tried and tested methods are used. *Looking after Corporate Health* brings together information on all aspects of health at work. It provides guidance on how to define problems and how to manage preventive measures. It rightly adopts a critical approach to the techniques discussed and should become a standard reference source for all good managers.

Health is a personal issue which arouses strong emotions; every organisation can benefit by ensuring that health problems are tackled before they become crises leading to industrial relations problems or a failure to comply with health and safety law. More positively, good healthcare at work will improve morale, aid the organisation's public image and help it to recruit and retain high quality staff. Good health is indeed good business, while bad health can be severely damaging and even fatal to an organisation.

Dr J. T. Carter,
Director of Medical Services,
The Health & Safety Executive.

Foreword

by **John Banham**
Director-General, Confederation of British Industry

People are central to the success of every business; they are the only source of sustainable competitive advantage. Companies which succeed have positive well-established policies for managing them.

Managers must take the lead in creating an environment where the full potential of every employee can be realised and rewarded.

The creation of a flexible, motivated workforce involves providing opportunities at all levels and in all functions, under-pinned by an equal opportunities policy. This benefits individuals and businesses and makes the best use of the skills and talents of the workforce.

The environment in which people work is of fundamental importance. Healthy and safe working surroundings mean high quality standards of protection and performance and ensure the well-being of all those in the workplace.

In addition corporate healthcare encourages healthy work and lifestyle practices. Not only are these beneficial for the individual but also contribute to lower absenteeism, improved performance and higher morale. Sickness absence alone costs British business well over £5 billion a year.

These comprehensive, practical books use the examples of a large number of companies and are designed for day-to-day use by personnel managers. Each book considers the value of the programmes, benefits to be gained, practical implementation and the costs involved.

CHAPTER 1

Introduction

The idea of employers taking an interest in the health and well-being of their employees took root at the beginning of the nineteenth century. Early employment legislation set the pattern which was to govern the thinking of responsible employers for many decades. But it was limited in two respects – it concentrated on the prevention of accidents rather than the protection of health, and it was concerned only with problems arising directly as a result of work.

The increasing pace of change in employee attitudes and technological innovation in recent years, has resulted in new thinking about the role of the employer as a provider of healthcare services. It has become clear that the major causes of employee illness, absenteeism, and premature death are not directly related to work. Nevertheless, the employer is in a unique position to contribute to the health and fitness of the workforce – with benefits for both employer and employees.

The employer about to introduce a corporate healthcare programme is faced with a wide range of options. To ensure effectiveness and value for money, the programme must be relevant to the employees in question, and must address real priorities.

Background

Why should organisations take an interest in the health of their employees? It is easy enough to think of some reasons why they should not – 'it's none of the employer's business', 'companies have to be concerned with profit', 'health is the responsibility of doctors'. However, the fact is that more and more organisations are becoming actively involved in the health of their workforce, and clearly believe it makes good business sense. Pick any of the UK's most successful companies, and you are likely to find some form of corporate health programme. This will have a committed budget, possibly some dedicated staff, and defined goals and objectives. This book is about why they bother, how they go about it, and what they achieve.

History

In historical terms, the idea of an employer taking any interest at all in the well-being of employees is quite new. Although there have no doubt always been enlightened and humanitarian employers, in the last century the norm was exploitation (at any rate, by today's standards). People were a straightforward resource, paid to do the job, and then left to look after themselves. At the beginning of the nineteenth century, no legislation anywhere in the world placed any restrictions in the terms and conditions employers created for their employees.

However, some courageous voices were being raised, protesting that the sheer cruelty of much employment – particularly of children – should not be allowed to continue. Notable amongst the reformers was the seventh Earl of Shaftesbury, Anthony Ashley Cooper. Shaftesbury was supported by publicists like Charles Dickens, but generally faced strident opposition from factory owners and the like. Nevertheless, there were some momentous achievements. In 1847 the ten hour day for factory workers was introduced. The Coal Mines Act of 1842 ended the employment of women in mines and of children under 13. The Climbing Boys Act of 1840 abolished the employment of children as chimney sweeps.

Collectively, the employment legislation developed during the nineteenth century was known as the Factory Acts. The very first was the Health and Morals of Apprentices Act of 1802. Originally concerned mainly with the employment of children, the Factory Acts progressively encompassed the control of workplace hazards – starting with the compulsory fencing-off of dangerous machinery in cotton mills. The latest such Act – the Factories Act of 1961 – is still in force, and regulates a range of workplace hazards. There are still requirements for fencing, now more commonly known as guarding, as well as stipulations regarding the provision of ventilation, safe access, entry into confined spaces, and the safety of lifting equipment.

By the middle of this century, the Factories Act approach had become widely accepted. The vigorous opposition of employers had subsided to occasional grumbling. A profession – that of the Safety Officer – had emerged to ensure implementation of the Factories Act, and most Safety Officers had impressive, almost encyclopaedic knowledge of the legislation. All the more surprising then, that the next real body of opposition to the Factories Act came from within the profession itself. This essentially started with a simple recognition that the legacy of Factories Acts, though worthy, was no longer achieving very much. Accident rates were static, and in many industries were unacceptably high. To investigate this problem, and make recommendations for action, a Government Committee of Enquiry was set up. The Committee was chaired by Lord Alfred Robens, ex-head of the Coal Board.

The Robens Report

Lord Robens reported the findings of his committee in 1972. The observations and conclusions were far reaching, and paved the way for a completely new approach to the protection of employees at work. In summary, his findings were as follows:

- Not only were accident and death rates unacceptably high, but they were regarded with universal apathy. Neither employers nor employees placed reduction of employment risks high on their list of priorities.
- The impressive volume of employment legislation which was embodied in the Factories Act, had become counter productive. When faced with an employment hazard, employers no longer asked 'is it safe?', but 'is it legal?' Many blatant hazards were being left untouched because they were not technically illegal – company lawyers concentrated on finding legal loopholes, rather than dealing with danger.
- The Factories Act approach was not capable of coping with the pace of change of modern industry and commerce. New technologies were being introduced at an unprecedented rate, and it was simply impossible to adjust the Act to accommodate the hazards of every new development.
- The nineteenth century approach had led to an obsession with *safety* rather than *health*. This was understandable, since the hazards of working with powerful machines or at heights are obvious to everyone, whilst the slow, insidious poisoning from airborne chemicals can take many years to identify. Nevertheless, evidence was growing that the obviousness of acute safety hazards was deflecting attention from the real priority – and that health should become the key subject for those dealing with workplace risks.

The Health and Safety at Work Act

The Robens Report went well beyond itemising what was wrong with the current situation. It set out a strategy for future action, and detailed proposals for new legislation. With relatively little disagreement, the report was accepted as the basis for a legislative review and resulted directly in the enactment of the Health and Safety at Work Act, 1974. This Act sharply changed approaches to the protection of employees from the hazards of work, and set the scene for a whole range of health considerations to become major corporate issues.

The Health and Safety at Work Act is dealt with in detail in the next chapter. Its enormous importance results from some fundamental changes from the pattern set for 150 years:

- it introduced 'general' duties for employers to protect employees, irrespective of what was causing the hazard;
- it clearly established that protection of health was just as important as the maintenance of safety;
- it required employers and employees to work out their own arrangements for health and safety at work;
- it introduced communication requirements, so that everyone should be properly informed and trained;
- it emphasised the importance of behavioural factors – controlling the acts of employees as well as the conditions of the workplace;
- it applied, almost without exception, to all places of work.

Occupational health

The background summary given so far may suggest that the first awareness of health as a corporate issue resulted from the arrival of the Health and Safety at Work Act. Nothing could be further from the truth. Indeed, workplace health has a longer history than workplace safety. A seventeenth century Italian physician, Bernardino Ramazzini, is generally credited with being the 'father' of occupational medicine. He noted that many of his patients developed illnesses which were a characteristic of the work they did. Writing of sewage workers, he said that the effects of work were 'equally troublesome as to be struck blind'. In his book *De Morbis Artificum Diatriba* (1700), he advised that, in addition to the questions that Hippocrates recommended, patients should be asked about their occupation.

After this impressive start, occupational health seems to have gone into rather a lull. Certainly the formulation of the Factories Acts focused around safety rather than health issues, and it is only relatively recently that occupational health has moved into the forefront. There are probably two fundamental reasons for its late arrival.

Firstly, tackling health hazards involves dealing with *chronic* rather than *acute* issues. Everyone understands and agrees about safety problems. The risk of, say, an unguarded machine severing a limb, is obvious and immediate. The action to reduce the risk is likely to meet with widespread support. The same is not true, however, for chronic health problems resulting from repeated exposure to airborne contaminants. Here, the risk is not at all obvious. Atmospheric contamination is usually invisible, odour-free, and produces no short-term ill-effects. There can be a delay of many years between first exposure and first symptoms – by which time it may be too late. In addition, occupational diseases such as dermatitis and asthma produce symptoms also seen in the non-occupational setting. As a result, it has required the emergence of the science of epidemiology – the study of the frequency and causes of diseases – to produce enough information for companies to clearly understand occupational health risks and to devise effective risk control strategies.

A good example of the slow emergence of occupational health awareness is asbestos. At the beginning of this century, asbestos dust was regarded as nothing more than a nuisance. A Home Office survey in 1911 showed no 'evidence of the existence of a serious health hazard in the industry'. In 1928 a case of non-tubercular fibrosis of the lungs in an asbestos worker prompted a further investigation, and dust control regulations were introduced, although no alarm was caused about the future of the industry. By the 1960s the link between asbestos exposure and fatal cancers was firmly established, and the powerful contribution of cigarette smoking to the risk was becoming understood. The problem was essentially the long latent period of the disease which, with this and other occupational exposures, served to mask the connection between cause and effect. A well known victim was the actor Steve McQueen who had a successful career in show business before succumbing to mesothelioma, contracted some 40 years earlier from working with asbestos.

Practitioners attempting to introduce the complex issues of chronically induced occupational disease into the workplace were not helped by the general attitudes to health and safety which were prevalent – even within the profession. These were summed up by the slogan 'health and safety is just a matter of common sense'. Perhaps this was an attempt to reassure people. In practice it resulted in complacency all round and deflected attention from the serious issues presented by chronic health hazards. The fact is that the hazards of work which presented much the greatest threat to life were completely inaccessible to 'common sense', and have involved the learning of new skills by everyone – employers, employees, and specialists.

With the benefit of hindsight, it is possible to see a second reason for the relatively slow emergence of occupational health. It is that occupational health is a *multi-disciplinary* profession, as indicated in Figure 1.1. It is very unlikely that a work-induced health problem can be tackled by a single individual. They simply will not have the necessary range of skills. Effective resolution could require the professional skills of doctors, engineers, trainers, hygienists, designers, accountants, lawyers, ergonomists, epidemiologists – to name but a few! However, our business (and indeed academic) culture rarely encourages real professional collaboration. Professions tend to zealously guard their skills, and often resent the input of others. As a consequence when, say, a company assembles its Medical Department, Works Engineers, Personnel Department, and Safety Advisers to tackle an issue such as noise-induced deafness, as much time can be consumed deciding who is in charge as in solving the problem.

This may seem critical, but it is meant as an observation rather than a judgement; we have all been guilty of over representation of our own interests. However, it is worth noting that too many professional interests tend to inhibit the effective development of subjects within organisations. This is relevant to the whole field of corporate healthcare, and must be addressed in any development strategies.

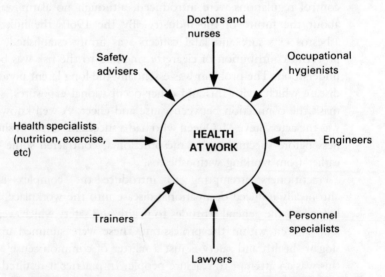

Figure 1.1 A multi-discipline approach is required to deal with health issues at work

Problems aside, the discipline of occupational health has emerged strongly in recent years. Indeed, it has had to – asbestos is far from the only workplace contaminant which has turned out to have serious health risks after being assumed to be harmless. Others to which responsible employers have had to turn their attention include beta napthylamine, vinyl chloride monomer, benzene, and many others. Other, non-chemical occupational health issues taking the stage in recent years include noise, vibration, and repetitive movement. In general, the profession which has co-ordinated the necessary skills is that of Occupational Hygiene – a narrow sounding name for a broadly based discipline. Occupational Hygienists specialise in the identification and measurement of workplace health risks, and then devising and implementing the measures necessary for risk minimisation.

Other professional disciplines have, of course, been involved in the development and implementation of workplace health practices. Medical practitioners contribute on many fronts, and are represented by bodies such as the Society of Occupational Medicine. Medical research has resulted in findings about environmental hazards which are central to the development of healthy work procedures. The nursing profession, through occupational health trained nurses, is in the front line of providing workplace health services – from basic treatment and first aid, to sophisticated health surveillance and professional counselling. Many engineering skills have been brought to bear on workplace health. Indeed without engineers, much occupational health would have to be reactive rather than preventive – it is usually the lot of engineers to clean up the environment, with dust extraction systems, acoustic enclosures, chemical filters and so on. Other vital skills are those of the professional communicators – supervisors, managers, trainers, personnel specialists. As has been said, health hazards at work are often not obvious, and considerable communication and persuasion skills are needed to introduce new procedures which may well be inconvenient and uncomfortable, and which produce no short-term tangible benefits – you just stay well.

The need for specialist professions to work together on workplace health, sometimes against their inclination, has produced various corporate institutions designed to ensure co-ordination. Inevitably, these are enshrined in the committee. The health and safety committee received official sanction with enactment of the Safety Representatives and Safety Committee Regulations in 1977. This legislation, introduced under the Health and Safety at Work Act, made health and safety committees mandatory if requested by trade union appointed safety representatives. Strictly speaking, the reasoning behind this legislation was that the workforce had a right to be informed about the hazards of their work, and consulted about risk reduction measures. However, the emphasis given to the committee was strongly related to the growing complexity of workplace health issues, the enormous volume of information which employers and employees had to handle, and the need for a whole range of individuals to come together and co-ordinate their activities if real improvements were to be seen in health standards. The new Regulations did not, of course, invent the health and safety committee. But they did result in its proliferation and many dire predictions were made about the time wasting which would result, with the 'talking-shops' taking over at the cost of decisive management action. The worst fears have not been realised, and such committees have actually played a real part in the growing understanding of complex health issues by a wide range of individuals.

Safety vs. Health

The historical background described so far has shown strong links between health and safety, whilst indicating that they have generally been regarded as separate subjects. Their connection is obvious, but their differences are important. As discussed earlier, the interests of safety are essentially the avoidance of *acute* threats to life and limb, i.e. the prevention of accidents. Health, on the other hand, is usually concerned with *chronic* events which develop over a period of time. Health is about the prevention of disease and the maintenance of well-being. From the point of view of devising corporate strategy, the distinction is to some extent academic. If the aim is to keep employees alive and well, then both health and safety have to be accommodated – and the priority at any time is the step which will achieve the greatest benefit (i.e. the greatest reduction in risk of injury, illness or death). In practice, this prioritising is often difficult. As has been said, professionals will generally advocate their own discipline, and will find it hard to take a detached, objective view if this results in their particular interest taking second place. Also, comparing health with safety is often not a matter of comparing like with like – the benefits of investing in one may be long term, and the other short term.

However, against this dilemma, one observation emerges strongly from the development of the subjects over the last few decades. It is the growing recognition that, contrary to 'common-sense' observation, the *health* hazards of most places of work have accounted for far more suffering, absenteeism, and death, than their safety hazards.

Work in coal mines resulted in more deaths from pneumoconiosis than from accidents, and the same was true of many industries – especially if they involved contact with chemicals. Death from chronic illness was often not associated with the victim's employment, because of the long delay between the exposure and the effect. Once under way, this awareness grew rapidly, and the priority of health and safety practitioners switched to the prevention of chronic illness. This was reflected in legislation which introduced requirements for the testing and labelling of chemicals, the provision of information about the hazards of substances used at work and much else. Recent examples of legislation to control chronic health hazards are the Noise at Work Regulations, 1989, and the so-called COSHH Regulations, 1988, (the acronym standing for the Control of Substances Hazardous to Health). The growing awareness of work-induced ill-health has caused a revolution in the practice of health and safety – and we are still in the midst of it. Findings about the health hazards of work still come thick and fast, resulting in the regular revision of exposure limits for chemicals used at work. There is no end in sight to legislation seeking to further reduce workplace health problems – laws to govern the use of visual display units, and to control hazardous manual handling, are anticipated at the time of writing. It is remarkable to note that this new legislation is being introduced under the regime of the Health and Safety at Work Act. This was an Act designed to eliminate the need for the constant introduction of new legislation. It was said that its 'general duties' would always accommodate new concerns and new findings, and that there would be no need for legislative detail of the sort that bedevilled the Factories Acts. The fact is that the complexity of modern occupational health issues simply demanded the precise standards that only legislation could provide. However, the development of such precision in the area of chronically induced illness proved far from straightforward. An example will illustrate the problems.

Noise-induced deafness

For most of this century it has been recognised that certain occupations are associated with deafness. Examples are shipbuilding and boiler-making, where it was accepted that workers were likely to become progressively more deaf over the years that their work continued. However, there is a difference between common observation of an illness associated with a particular group, and actually establishing cause and effect. It was some time before the true nature of the problem became clear, but in the early 1960s it was established beyond doubt that the deafness was the result of prolonged exposure to excessive noise.

Noise-induced deafness is a classic occupational disease. Limited exposure to noise does little harm. Any effect on hearing is usually temporary, and the ears are back to normal within a few hours. However, if the noise exposure is repeated or is prolonged, damage is caused to the sound-sensitive cells buried deep in the inner ear. Each human ear has about 30,000 such cells, and a day's exposure to typical industrial noise will probably only destroy a few of them. There is therefore no detectable impairment to hearing, and no apparent reason to take any protective or avoidance action.

At work though, the daily exposure is repeated, and every day more hearing cells are lost. After several years the worker may begin to feel that sounds are becoming muffled. He may complain that people no longer speak as clearly as they used to. As more years pass, the deafness starts to become a real handicap. Everyday conversation turns into a struggle, and the individual may appear to become reclusive and unsociable. Simple tasks which involve conversation, such as shopping, become difficult, and the victim retreats more and more into his own world. To compound the handicap, the noise-induced deafness is likely to be associated with other unpleasant effects. The most common is tinnitus, or 'ringing in the ears'. Many victims would happily settle for total deafness, if only they could, rather than live with the endless disruptive din of tinnitus.

Sadly, noise-induced deafness is neither curable nor correctable. The destroyed hearing cells will not regenerate, and cannot be replaced by surgery. Worse still, noise-induced deafness is not usually helped by hearing aids. The reason for this is that deafness caused by noise particularly affects hearing at a certain frequency – generally around 4000–6000 Hertz, resulting in apparent distortion of sound. A hearing aid merely amplifies the distorted sound – it cannot restore hearing in the lost frequencies.

Given the severity of the disability, and the unarguable knowledge in the 1960s that it was caused by noise exposure at work, the solution would seem clear – limit workplace noise exposure by law. Why then did it take more than 20 years for such legislation to emerge? The answer reveals the inherent problems of dealing with chronic ill health caused by work.

Dose-response relationship
Nearly all health effects resulting from environmental or occupational

exposures show a **dose-response** relationship. In other words, the more you are exposed to the hazard, the more likely you are to experience the illness – or the more severely you will experience its effects. Figure 1.2 shows a dose-response relationship for exposure to noise. The units along the horizontal axis show the average noise level to which a group of workers are exposed throughout their working lives. The vertical axis shows how many people will have suffered serious hearing disablement as a result of that exposure. As you can see, the louder the noise the more people become deaf. This unsurprising observation applies to most chronically induced illness – and thwarts the development of occupational health standards, and the introduction of legislation. Somehow an almost impossible decision has to be made – how many people should the legislation (or the occupational health standard) protect? The first reaction is obvious; the standard should protect everyone. But consider the implications of a noise standard set on that basis. The graph shows that, even at the quite low

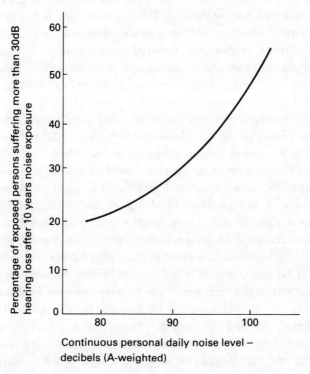

Figure 1.2   Dose-response relationship for exposure to noise

noise level of 80 decibels, a small percentage of the exposed population will become deaf. And, desirable though it might be for the standard to protect those individuals, it is simply not realistic; industrial noise could not technically be reduced to such levels. To tackle the problem with hearing protectors such as ear muffs would involve almost the entire working population wearing protectors, since you do not know who the especially noise-sensitive individuals are until it is too late.

The reality facing this, and nearly all other workplace health issues, is that we must settle for compromise. A balance has to be struck between the desire to protect as many people as possible, and the need to be technically and commercially realistic. This often results in heated debate and, in the case of noise, the debate lasted for 20 years. To somewhat over-simplify, the debate was between employers (particularly represented by the CBI), and employees (represented by the TUC). Employers wanted the legal noise limit to be as high as possible (at least 90 decibels), so that the cost to industry would not be crippling. Employees, on the other hand, wanted as low a limit as possible (ideally less than 85 decibels), in order to protect the largest possible number of workers. The debate might still be continuing if a European Directive had not intervened. This set a deadline for noise legislation in member countries and, as a result, limits were set. As with many compromises, both parties achieved some honour. The main requirements for noise control are introduced at 90 decibels, but some actions relating to making ear protectors available are mandatory at 85 decibels.

Noise-induced deafness has been used to illustrate some typical characteristics of chronic illness caused by work. A similar story could be told for almost any occupational disease. First, casual observation links a disease with an occupation. Statistical studies and epidemiology confirm the observation and give an indication of its magnitude. Research work, possibly involving animal tests, produces dose-response data (showing how much exposure is needed to cause the illness). Intense debate takes place to decide what workplace standard should be set, invariably involving compromise between a level which would protect everyone (which might involve banning the substance altogether), and a level which can be achieved with minimum disruption to business. This process has become commonplace. It has been accelerated by the Health and Safety at Work Act, by European Directives, and by pressure from employees taking a growing interest in their health, and expecting to be informed and involved in matters which directly affect them. However, whilst this movement was gathering pace, another was moving alongside.

General health

It has been observed that a comparison of accident risks with illness risks, shows that control of health hazards offers more scope for protecting employees than control of safety hazards. This has been the case since the Industrial Revolution at the end of the eighteenth century, when machines and power arrived, and exposed large populations to environmental conditions with which the human body was not designed to cope. Recognition of the importance of health hazards, which now seems so obvious, came slowly but has resulted in a frequent *prioritising* of health issues so that resource can be directed where it will have most effect. This prioritising leads inevitably to an observation which is of great importance to all employers. It is that ill health *not* caused by work, results in far more disruption to business than ill health which *is* caused by work.

Later chapters will consider the statistics in detail, but it is worth asking the question, 'what is the major cause of serious illness and premature death amongst employees in the average company?' The answer is not something resulting from workplace hazards, it is heart disease. After heart disease comes motor accidents. Now comes the question which is at the centre of much debate about corporate healthcare programmes. 'Is the observation that general health issues affect more employees than occupational health issues, of merely academic interest to employers, or should they do something about it?' Some organisations have taken the view that they should not become involved in issues for which they have no responsibility – it is simply regarded as none of their business. For some the idea of an involvement in general health and well-being conjures images of old style, paternalistic management, with the factory owner involving himself in almost every aspect of his employees' lives. However, more and more organisations are taking the subject of general employee health very seriously indeed. Here are some of the reasons:

- it is in the employer's commercial interests – employees who are absent with heart disease are just as absent as those who are away with work-induced illness, and resource directed to reducing heart disease could make business sense;
- many common illnesses are essentially preventable, but people need to know how – employers are far and away the main educators of adults; employment-based training has a captive audience and is provided both as a need (work skills training), and as a legal duty (safety procedures,

etc.). Many employers accept that it is part of their responsibility to bring health education messages to their employees;

- most employers genuinely care for their employees, and wish to be seen to care – providing a health service is a clear sign of that commitment;
- some health issues which seem at first to have little to do with work, actually contain some workplace component – heart disease, for example, may partly result from the stress of employment, and from high fat food eaten in the works canteen;
- employees increasingly demand healthcare as part of their employment package – skilled employees are an ever more scarce resource and can often afford to be choosy about their employers; the quality of healthcare offered by an employer is a good test of the quality of the employer, and a tax-effective way to receive benefit.

Professional anxiety

This book does not assume that the reader automatically supports corporate health programmes. But it does assume that they are at least not automatically opposed to them. The aim of the book is to review some of the options, to consider the pros and cons of alternative courses of action, and to look at the experience of others who have already introduced healthcare programmes at work.

As with so many aspects of employee protection programmes, the idea of introducing general health issues into the workplace raises some professional eyebrows. For many, the strict discipline of 'occupational health' relates only to illness caused by the conditions of employment. This is perhaps understandable, since this is a complex area of science with its own techniques, terminology, and practitioners. The term occupational health therefore needs to be used with care. However, the eminence of the science does not need to preclude the introduction of broader health issues into work, or indeed mean that this will not sometimes be the priority.

Perhaps the occasional professional anxiety about this field of activity relates not so much to its legitimacy, as to the way in which general employee healthcare first became a significant area of business. This was with the arrival of the so-called 'executive medical'. Executive health screening is a relatively expensive employment perk, often justified on the grounds that senior executives are expensive to replace and therefore screening is worth the money if it keeps the executives alive and well. Such screens usually involve a wide range of medical tests, often undertaken in luxurious clinics. However, as a *first* step in introducing healthcare to companies, they can be criticised on two main grounds.

The first is the inevitable implication that executives must be more prone to illness than the population at large to justify the disproportionate expenditure on their health. The reality is that, by almost any yardstick you care to choose, executives are *more* healthy than the rest of the population. The second criticism is that spending a large amount of money to screen relatively few people means that some of the tests undertaken are likely to be of questionable value. Health screening, like everything else, suffers from the law of diminishing returns. The first pound is extremely well spent, but the two hundredth will probably be giving less useful information. The allocation of health screening resource will be considered in detail in Chapter 3, but it is worth acknowledging that the introduction of executive health screening has not always met with the approval of employees or healthcare professionals, and has sometimes set back the introduction of more broadly based services.

Options

So, executive screening aside, what other options are open to employers who wish to contribute to the health of their employees? They fall into five main categories:

1. *Treatment*. All companies are required to ensure that first aid treatment is available following injuries, but a wide range of additional treatment can be offered. For sufficiently large companies, this can include on-site doctors, dentists, physiotherapists, opticians, chiropodists, etc. Companies often fund private medical treatment undertaken in hospitals, usually by paying the premiums for private health insurance.
2. *Screening*. Many screening services are available to employers. They include specific tests such as blood cholesterol, urine testing, etc., as well as combinations of tests making up coronary screening, well woman screening, etc.
3. *Health education*. Many health problems can be alleviated or avoided, provided there is knowledge about what needs to be done, and support where necessary. Health education can take many forms, from formal training to light-hearted campaigns. Education can be direct to the employee, or indirect – for example by training managers – to spot the early signs of stress.
4. *Counselling*. Health problems, especially if they relate to stress or

addiction, may need professional counselling if they are to be tackled effectively. Counselling can be provided by suitably trained people within the organisation, by external specialists, or through a fully-blown Employee Assistance Programme.

5. *Facilities*. Companies can provide a range of healthcare facilities, or can fund access to external facilities. These can include gymnasia and health clubs. There may also be scope for making existing facilities, such as canteens, more health-oriented.

Subsequent chapters will consider these options in detail, and review the sort of costs and benefits which can be anticipated. However, it is perhaps worth closing this chapter with some thoughts about the ultimate objectives of corporate healthcare programmes. Reduced to basics, any company health initiatives should probably meet at least one, and probably both of the following objectives. First, any action should genuinely contribute to the health of employees, and not just pay lip-service to the concept. Second, the programme should contribute to the overall aims of the organisation – which may include quality standards, market leadership and, with few exceptions, making a profit.

In considering any health initiatives, applying the following questions might help to clarify whether it is worth proceeding:

- Does the proposal address the real health priorities for our employees?
- Have we set clear health performance objectives for the service, and will there be measurement to show whether those objectives have been met?
- Have all costs involved definitely been anticipated and accepted?
- Will financial savings be measured and monitored?
- If external suppliers are involved, will they provide adequate quality and professionalism at the right price?
- Are we making maximum use of any data which is obtained (eg statistical analysis of results and trends)?
- Do our proposals include communicating details to the workforce in the most effective way?
- Are we fully complying with all relevant legal requirements?
- Do our proposals have the support of employees and their representatives?
- Do our proposals have the commitment of senior management – and is this seen to be the case?

CHAPTER 2
Law and Corporate Health

The Health and Safety at Work Act 1974 makes it the responsibility of all employers to ensure not only the safety, but also the health and welfare at work of their employees.

Since 1974, the Act has been reinforced by further legislation, typically in the form of detailed regulations dealing with a specific workplace hazard – e.g. lead, asbestos and ionising radiation.

Most recently the Control of Substances Hazardous to Health (COSHH) and the Noise at Work Regulations have added to the legal requirements on the safeguarding of employees' health. In particular, the employer is required to adopt an approach which identifies, assesses, controls and monitors potential health hazards in the workplace.

This legislation is mainly enforced by the Health and Safety Executive and by local authorities. At the same time, an employee whose ill health results from work may well be able to pursue a claim for financial compensation (damages) in the civil courts.

New legislation in this field is increasingly initiated at a European rather than at a national level.

The revolutionary act

Now that the Health and Safety at Work Act 1974 has been in force for some years, it is easy to forget just how revolutionary it was when it was introduced. Never before had there been in the UK a single Act of Parliament which applied to everyone at work, regardless of the type of workplace or the process/activity carried out there. The Act protected anyone whose health or safety is put at risk by people at work, regardless of whether they were an employee, a visitor, a contractor, a local resident, and it covers the whole range of hazards encountered in the workplace.

The Act is not simply concerned with safety. Section 1 of the Act makes it clear that the objective is also to secure the health and welfare of people at work, and to protect anyone else from a risk to health arising from people who are at work. Major responsibilities for employee health are created by the Act, and a special duty falls on the employer. Under section 2, the employer must ensure the health, safety and welfare of all his employees, so far as is reasonably practicable. In particular the employer must look at:

- provision and maintenance of plant and systems of work;
- use, handling, storage and transport of articles and substances;
- provision of information, instruction, training and supervision;
- maintaining a safe place of work, and safe access; and
- provision and maintenance of a safe working environment.

Within each of these points, the Act emphasises health just as strongly as safety, and this dual emphasis is maintained in other key sections of the Act.

Section 3 deals with the employer's duty to non-employees, and with the responsibility of self employed people for their own health and safety − and for that of other people. Section 4 deals with the special responsibilities of those 'in control of non-domestic premises', while Section 6 is concerned with the responsibilities of designers, manufacturers, suppliers, erectors and installers.

Section 7 sets out the responsibility of individual employees.

However, although the Act talks about health just as much as safety, in practice it is the safety implications which have received far more attention than the health ones. Two reasons for this are:

1. Safety problems are generally far easier to identify, assess and control than health problems. Dealing with an unguarded machine is more straightforward than dealing with a noise problem. Equally, it is much easier for a personnel manager to respond to an employee who complains of a defective ladder than to someone who is unhappy about working at a VDU for long periods, or who complains about the general working environment, or who is concerned about a possible outbreak of Legionnaire's disease.

2. Health and safety advice has traditionally been given by people who are safety specialists rather than health specialists. They naturally feel far more comfortable with safety rather than with health issues.

However, since the 1974 Act the balance of interest has shifted away from safety towards health. The principal reasons for this are:

- the introduction of specific legislation requiring employers to act on health issues, the most significant examples being the Control of Substances Hazardous to Health (COSHH) Regulations 1988 and the Noise at Work Regulations 1989;
- tied in with the first point, a steady stream of EC legislation concerned with health issues in the workplace;
- a heightened awareness among employees of health matters generally, coupled with raised expectations about the level of healthcare provided by the employer;
- pressure from employee groups such as trade unions;
- a general recognition that, in terms of both lost time and preventable premature death, health issues are probably at least ten times as important as safety issues.

In the remainder of this chapter, we set out the most significant legal developments in the post-Health and Safety at Work Act period, with particular comment on COSHH and the Noise at Work Regulations, and identify some of the key issues for managers.

COSHH

Since the 1974 Act, the Government has introduced a number of pieces of legislation dealing with specific workplace hazards to health. These include:

- the Control of Lead at Work Regulations 1980 – these rationalised and strengthened earlier law on exposure to lead and introduced into the law for the first time the concept that the employer should make a formal assessment of the health hazard to his employees, and then introduce and maintain whatever control measures the assessment showed to be necessary;
- the Classification, Packaging and Labelling of Dangerous Substances Regulations 1984, which among other things brought the UK more into line with EC and international conventions on the labelling of dangerous goods, whether used at work or not;
- a series of regulations about asbestos, introducing a licensing scheme for contractors and others involved in work with asbestos lagging and insulation, prohibiting the use of asbestos for certain purposes, requiring asbestos products to be labelled and introducing a regime for

controlling employees' exposure to asbestos similar to that brought in for lead workers by the Control of Lead at Work Regulations (see above);

- the Ionising Radiations Regulations 1985 – these technically complex Regulations introduced new requirements for people's protection against ionising radiation in the workplace (alpha particles, beta particles, gamma rays, X-rays etc.). They stress the need to prevent/minimise people's exposure to radiation – e.g. through the application of expert advice, sound design/engineering and the use of safe systems of work. They do *not* cover non-ionising radiation such as radiowaves, microwaves, infra-red and ultra-violet light.

However, the most important of all of these is the Control of Substances Hazardous to Health Regulations 1988 – COSHH.

What substances are covered?

COSHH applies to substances arising out of work under the employer's control which meet one or more of the following criteria:

- they are classified as very toxic, toxic, corrosive, harmful or irritant for supply purposes in the 'Approved List' under the Classification, Packaging and Labelling of Dangerous Substances Regulations 1984;
- they are substances for which a Maximum Exposure Limit (MEL) or an Occupational Exposure Standard (OES) has been set. MELs are listed in a Schedule to COSHH and both MELs and OESs are listed in HSE Guidance Note EH40, which is revised annually;
- they are dusts of any kind, present in 'substantial concentration' (defined in COSHH);
- they are micro-organisms which can cause illness;
- they are any other substance with a comparable hazard.

For easy reference, any substance labelled with one of the signs shown in Figure 2.1 is likely to be a 'substance hazardous to health':

Exceptions

The definition of 'substance' is very broad. Solids, liquids, gases, fumes, vapours and micro-organisms are all specifically included. The scope of COSHH is extremely wide, but some substances are excluded, notably because they are already covered by legislation which is similar in approach to COSHH. The main examples of substances not covered

---

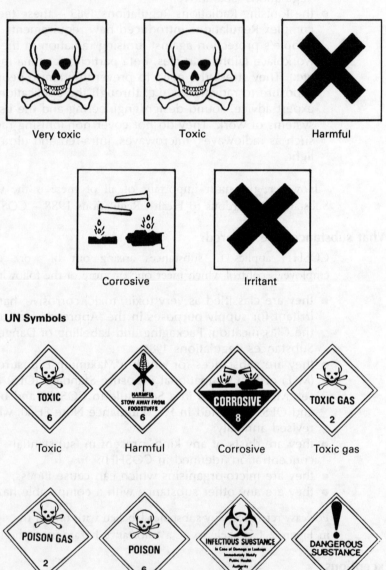

EC Symbols

Very toxic

Toxic

Harmful

Corrosive

Irritant

UN Symbols

TOXIC 6

Toxic

HARMFUL STOW AWAY FROM FOODSTUFFS 6

Harmful

CORROSIVE 8

Corrosive

TOXIC GAS 2

Toxic gas

POISON GAS 2

Poison gas

POISON 6

Poison

INFECTIOUS SUBSTANCE In Case of Damage or Leakage Immediately Notify Public Health Authority 6

Infectious substance

DANGEROUS SUBSTANCE

Other dangerous substance

Figure 2.1 Substances hazardous to health will often be labelled with one, or a combination of the above warning symbols

by COSHH are:

- lead (covered by the Control of Lead at Work Regulations 1980);
- asbestos (covered by the Control of Asbestos at Work Regulations 1987 and various other provisions);
- substances which are only hazardous because they are
  - radioactive
  - explosive or flammable
  - at high pressure
  - hot or cold; and
- substances administered as part of medical treatment.

What does COSHH require?

COSHH puts into statutory form five basic principles of occupational health management. These are:

1. Assessment – the identification and analysis of hazards, and the selection of control measures.
2. Control – the implementation of measures which will prevent or minimise employee exposure to the hazardous substances.
3. Maintenance – of the chosen control measures, to ensure they do in practice give the degree of protection deemed necessary by the assessment.
4. Monitoring – to check that control is adequate.
5. Information – so that all involved know what they are working with, what the hazards are and the precautions to take both in normal operation and an emergency, e.g. spills and leakage.

These are analysed in greater detail below.

1. THE COSHH ASSESSMENT

The requirement for assessment reflects the basic Health and Safety at Work Act principle that the prime responsibility for identifying, understanding, evaluating and controlling a hazard lies with the employer.

This recognises that no two workplaces are the same, and that even where identical materials are handled, there may be big differences in control systems and working methods – and hence in the resulting hazard to employees' health.

Thus the solvent 1,1,1-trichloroethane, classified and labelled as 'harmful', may create a range of risks. Used as a thinner in typewriter correction fluid in 20 ml containers it provides a negligible risk to

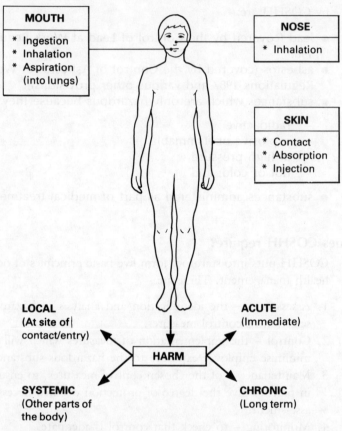

MOUTH
* Ingestion
* Inhalation
* Aspiration
  (into lungs)

NOSE
* Inhalation

SKIN
* Contact
* Absorption
* Injection

LOCAL
(At site of
contact/entry)

ACUTE
(Immediate)

HARM

SYSTEMIC
(Other parts of
the body)

CHRONIC
(Long term)

Figure 2.2   Harmful substances – routes of entry

health. But when used in large quantities as a cleaning solvent in a confined or poorly-ventilated place (e.g. inside a storage tank) by an
unprotected operator, it poses a serious risk to health, including possible unconsciousness or death.

It is therefore essential that the assessment takes into account not
only the inherent properties of a substance (the hazard) but also the
potential danger in the actual circumstances of use (the risk).

The assessment should therefore be a systematic review of:

● what is present;
● routes of entry into the body (see Figure 2.2) and possible
  harm;
● how substances are handled;
● who could be affected, and how much;
● the circumstances in which hazards arise;

- the likelihood of harm;
- what precautions are necessary.

The assessment must be 'suitable and sufficient' and should be in writing except in the simplest of cases. It must identify what action needs to be taken to comply with COSHH, and it must be communicated to employees. It must be reviewed and updated as necessary – for example because of changes in the process, such as new materials being taken into use, or because new information comes to light about the hazards of existing substances.

2. CONTROL

COSHH makes the following principles of control legally binding:

- exposure to hazardous substances should be prevented;
- where prevention is not reasonably practicable, exposure must be adequately controlled;
- prevention and/or control must be by means other than the provision of personal protective equipment (PPE) – again, so far as is reasonably practicable;
- where these measures still do not provide adequate protection, suitable PPE (e.g. respirators) must be provided and used.

In some cases, air sampling or some other form of monitoring will be needed to prove that control is adequate. Where the substance is one which has a set Maximum Exposure Limit or Occupational Exposure Standard, the monitoring results will need to be compared with the limit to decide whether adequate control is being maintained.

In this context 'controls' mean the measures taken to prevent or minimise exposure. These may include one or more of the following, with the most effective controls being those towards the top of the list:

- stop using the substance;
- use a less hazardous substance, or the same substance in a less hazardous form;
- totally enclose the process and handling systems;
- prevent or minimise the emission of dust/fume etc.;
- limit the area of contamination in the event of leaks and spills;
- partially enclose the process and use local exhaust ventilation (LEV);
- use LEV without an enclosure;
- use general (dilution) ventilation;

- restrict the number of employees exposed and/or their exposure period;
- improve regular cleaning/decontamination;
- provide means for safe storage and disposal;
- provide suitable protective clothing/equipment;
- prohibit eating, drinking, smoking and the application of cosmetics in the contaminated area(s);
- improve washing and changing facilities.

3. THE USE AND MAINTENANCE OF CONTROLS

To be effective, controls have to be applied in practice and properly maintained. COSHH places specific duties on both the employer and the employee. The employer must take all reasonable steps to ensure the proper use of whatever control measures are adopted, while employees must make full and proper use of any equipment provided and report defects so that they can be put right.

In addition, the employer is required to make sure control measures are maintained 'in an efficient state, in efficient working order and in good repair'. To this end:

- all engineering controls (e.g. enclosed systems) must be thoroughly examined and tested at suitable intervals;
- local exhaust ventilation equipment must be thoroughly examined and tested at least once every 14 months (shorter intervals apply to certain specified processes);
- Respiratory Protective Equipment (RPE) – e.g. respirators and breathing apparatus – must be thoroughly examined (and tested, where appropriate) at suitable intervals – normally not exceeding three months. (One-shift disposable respirators are exempt from this requirement);
- records of these tests/examinations (and of any remedial work or repairs carried out as a result) must be kept for at least five years.

4. MONITORING

In the context of COSHH, monitoring means using techniques such as air sampling to measure employees' likely exposure to 'substances hazardous to health'. This may involve an operator wearing a sampling device to record exposure to a given substance, with the results being checked against set standards – such as Maximum Exposure Limits and Occupational Exposure Standards.

COSHH stipulates only two processes where monitoring is always required:

1. Work with vinyl chloride monomer (VCM). Frequency: continuous.
2. Where vapour/spray is given off from vessels in which an electrolytic chromium process is carried on. Frequency: every 14 days. (Trivalent chromium processes are exempt.)

But employees' exposure must also be monitored where it is requisite for ensuring the maintenance of adequate control measures, or it is otherwise requisite for protecting employees' health. It is part of the assessment to determine whether these criteria apply, and hence whether monitoring is needed.

Employees may have to be under 'health surveillance' which could involve a regular medical carried out by a doctor or suitably trained nurse. Employees may need to see an Employment Medical Advisor (EMA) or an HSE-Appointed Doctor. In some cases, health surveillance can be done by a non-medical person – e.g. a supervisor who regularly checks people's hands and arms for signs of dermatitis in activities in which dermatitis is a hazard.

Records of monitoring must be kept. Any personal record (e.g. monitoring or health surveillance) must be kept for 30 years. Other exposure records must be retained for at least five years.

5. INFORMATION AND TRAINING
People must know:

● what they are working with;
● what the hazards are;
● what precautions they need to take to work safely;
● what they should do in an emergency.

This will in practice involve a combination of information, instruction and training. Employees are entitled to know the result of any air monitoring carried out, and indeed the results of health surveillance (although in this case the information must be in such a form as to make it impossible to identify the results relating to any specific individual).

In addition to the COSHH Regulations themselves, there are three approved Codes of Practice and various guidance literature available from HMSO. Some free leaflets are also available through Health and Safety Executive Area Offices.

COSHH has received much comment and discussion, and a huge volume of literature is available. However, as with all complex packages, it is sometimes hard to keep the key principles at the front of one's mind.

Key points of COSHH for the manager

1. WIDE SCOPE

COSHH covers any workplace and (with a few technical exceptions) any 'substance hazardous to health'. Many raw materials, solvents, cleaning materials and wastes are included, as is anything labelled toxic, very toxic, corrosive, harmful or irritant.

2. ALL EXPOSURES MUST BE ASSESSED

The risks associated with a substance depend not only on its hazardous properties but on how it is used: how much, in what form, by whom, in what environment and under what control. COSHH prohibits any work which may expose someone to a substance hazardous to health unless a 'suitable and sufficient' assessment has taken place.

3. MATCHING THE RISK

The depth of the assessment, and the amount of resources applied to control, should be linked to the risk. Where the risk is small, the assessment can be simple and minimal resources applied to control. Conversely, where the risk is significant, the assessment needs to be more detailed and we have to be ready to spend more on eliminating or reducing the risk.

4. ASSESSMENT IS CONTINUING AND NOT ONE-OFF

We are required by law to review the initial assessment where e.g. process changes are made, different materials are used, or new information comes to light about existing materials. But we should in any case constantly re-appraise our processes and control methods to identify how risks could be eliminated or further reduced.

5. PREVENTION IS THE PRIORITY

The aim is to prevent anyone being exposed to a hazardous substance. Where this is not reasonably practicable, exposure must be controlled and minimised.

6. PERSONAL PROTECTIVE EQUIPMENT (PPE) IS THE LAST RESORT

PPE (including all forms of respiratory protective equipment) is only permissible where better control methods – such as engineering and process controls – are not reasonably practicable.

---

7. ALL COSHH WORK MUST BE RECORDED

We are legally required to keep records of COSHH assessments, environmental monitoring, inspection and maintenance of control systems and the health surveillance of individuals (where this is required). However, we should be able to demonstrate any aspect of our work on COSHH by reference to the appropriate documentation.

8. EVERYONE MUST KNOW WHAT THEY'RE DEALING WITH

We must ensure that staff at all levels have the necessary information to understand the hazards of substances to which they are or might be exposed. This might be by means of suitable labelling, other written information or direct instruction/training.

9. EVERYONE MUST KNOW HOW TO WORK SAFELY

People must know what precautions they need to take to ensure a safe working environment for themselves and others. For example, where appropriate, employees must understand how extract ventilation works and when to flag up that it is not working properly. Anyone who has to use personal protective equipment must know how to do so safely.

10. UNUSUAL EVENTS MUST BE CONSIDERED

The whole COSHH strategy of risk identification, assessment and control applies not only to normal operation but to any foreseeable situation. Abnormal but foreseeable events such as spillage and leakage of hazardous substances must be considered. Employees must know what to do if they happen.

Employer's response to COSHH

No new piece of health and safety legislation is introduced in the UK without extensive consultation with employers, trade unions and other interested parties. The introduction of COSHH was preceded by some years of consultation, and a number of the comments, suggestions and objections put forward at that stage influenced the final content of the Regulations.

This period of consultation also meant that employers had ample time to ponder the likely implications of COSHH for their own business or organisation. There was a wide range of reaction, as might well be expected given that the legislation was to require some action of virtually every employer.

However, within this range of reactions, two particular strands can be identified. First, some large organisations expressed the view that COSHH would not make much difference to them, as they had already been doing for years on a voluntary basis everything that was now to be made a legal requirement.

At the other end of the scale were those organisations who were uncomfortable about these new and far-reaching requirements and who believed that they would be used as a 'cosh' by the enforcing authorities.

As it has turned out, both were wrong. Those in the 'I'm all right Jack!' camp have found that while they might have been complying broadly with the approach and basic principles on which COSHH is based, there is much in the detail of the Regulations which has required them to take action which was not being taken before.

Two good examples concern assessments and Respiratory Protective Equipment (RPE). Many organisations followed the 'Assess-Control-Monitor' approach before COSHH came along, but it is fair to say that few had formalised and documented what they were doing to the extent now required. COSHH requires RPE – with the exception of the single-shift disposable respirator – to be regularly examined by a competent person and suitable records kept. Again, while it is fair to say that many companies realised the importance of proper mainten-ance for RPE, very few had arrangements which were so systematic and formal that they would without modification satisfy COSHH.

At the other end of the scale, COSHH has not proved to be the bludgeon that some organisations feared. The Health and Safety Executive did not suddenly swoop on 1 January 1990 (the deadline for completion of assessments on existing processes and activities) closing down companies right, left and centre because they had not finished their COSHH assessment. However there is evidence of a greater will-ingness on the HSE's part to use enforcement action, now that COSHH has been in force for some time.

There is no doubt that COSHH has called on companies and other organisations to commit significant time and other resources to setting up the systems necessary to comply. It is equally true that there are many small and medium-sized companies which have not identified COSHH's implications for them, and as time goes by, they must be increasingly vulnerable to enforcement action by the Health and Safety Executive and local authorities.

However, prompted by COSHH, many organisations have come to a better understanding of the health risks created by their operations. Sometimes it has been possible to minimise those risks very simply and cheaply. COSHH has given managers a structure for achieving a safe working environment in practice, and as implementation of COSHH proceeds, it will make the workplace a healthier one for all employees.

Noise

Until recently, there has been in the UK very little specific legislation to protect people from noise at work. However, on the 1 January 1990, Britain introduced the Noise at Work Regulations 1989, implementing EC Directive 86/188/EC.

The action required by the Regulations will depend on whether any of the defined 'action levels' are reached. These are as follows:

- first action level – 85 dB(A) LEP,d – i.e. a noise dose of 85 dB(A) for 8 hours or an equivalent dose, such as 88 dB(A) for 4 hours (the scale is logarithmic, so an increase of 3 dB(A) is a doubling of the level);
- second action level – 90 dB(A) LEP,d – i.e. a noise dose of 90 dB(A) for 8 hours or an equivalent dose, such as 96 dB(A) for 2 hours;
- peak action level – a peak sound pressure of 200 Pascals (140 dB).

A word of explanation about the decibel scale may help. The decibel is the basic unit for measuring noise intensity. The (A) scale is a special one used for measurement of noise in the workplace. It is 'weighted' to adjust for the fact that the ear's sensitivity varies according to the frequency (pitch) of the noise.

As a rough guide, if it is so noisy that it is necessary to shout to be heard by a person standing one metre away, the noise level is likely to be close to 90 dB(A). 85 dB(A) is considerably less noisy – it is the sort of level you would experience in busy road traffic.

What the regulations require

1. ASSESSMENT BY A COMPETENT PERSON

This applies where any employee is likely to be exposed at or above either the first action level or the peak action level. It means that a noise survey must be carried out to identify 'at risk' employees and noisy areas. The assessment must be reviewed and updated if circumstances change, and records must be kept of the assessment and of any later review.

2. ACTION TO MINIMISE RISK

Regulation 6 requires each employer to reduce the risk of noise-induced damage to employees' hearing to the lowest level reasonably practicable. It should be noted that 'exposure to noise' must be read as 'exposure to noise at work'. The employer is not obliged to take any steps to protect his employees from noise from other sources, e.g. discotheques, clay pigeon shooting, etc!

3. ACTION TO REDUCE EXPOSURE

Where any employee is likely to be exposed at or above the second action level, or the peak action level, the employer must reduce that exposure so far as is reasonably practicable. This must be by means other than the provision of personal ear protectors, e.g. reducing noise at source, enclosing noisy machinery, limiting the time employees spend in noisy areas.

4. PROVISION OF EAR PROTECTION

Where the daily exposure is likely to be 85 dB(A) or more, employees must be provided (on request) with personal ear protectors which are 'suitable and efficient'. Personal ear protectors must always be provided to any employee who is likely to be exposed at or above the second action level or peak action level.

5. EAR PROTECTION ZONES

The employer is required to identify and mark ear protection zones and ensure that no employee enters these zones unless he/she is wearing personal ear protectors. Ear protection zones are those in which any employee is likely to be exposed at or above the second action level or the peak action level. A suitable sign is shown in Figure 2.3.

6. MAINTENANCE AND USE OF EQUIPMENT

Regulation 10 places duties on both employer and employee regarding the full and proper use of anything (e.g. ear protectors) provided under the Regulations. In addition, the employer is obliged to maintain anything he provides ('in an efficient state, in efficient working order and in good repair'), while the employee is required to report any defect to the employer.

7. EDUCATION

Where employees are likely to be exposed at or above the first action level or the peak action level, the employer must provide each one with adequate information, instruction and training on:

● the risk of damage to that employee's hearing;

Figure 2.3 Ear protection zone sign

- what steps the employee can take to minimise risk;
- what the employee needs to do to obtain personal ear protectors;
- the employee's own obligations under the Regulations.

8. MANUFACTURERS ETC. OF ARTICLES FOR USE AT WORK

Manufacturers, suppliers and importers must provide information on noise levels, if the noise output (say, of a new machine) is such as to be likely to cause any employee to be exposed at or above the first action level or the peak action level.

Action plan

The following checklist can be used to structure action on noise:

- decide where a formal noise survey is necessary;
- ensure that the assessment is done by a competent person and that records are kept;
- consider control at source wherever possible;
- identify and mark ear protection zones;
- ensure ear protectors give the necessary degree of attenuation, and are as comfortable as possible;
- educate and train the workers affected;
- ensure that managers and supervisors understand the new requirements and take positive action to ensure compliance;
- monitor controls, systems and procedures to ensure they are operating effectively;
- update the assessment as necessary (e.g. changed processes, new machinery etc.).

Manual handling

Manual handling injuries are believed to account for more than 25 per cent of all reported work injuries and to cost well in excess of £100 million per year resulting from lost production and medical treatment.

Much debate has taken place concerning the form in which legislation should be drafted, the principal problems being large variations in individual lifting capacity, and the number of complicating factors which influence whether a lift is safe or not.

In 1982, the Health and Safety Commission published draft legislation based on four action categories, according to the weight being lifted, but the proposal was not progressed owing to criticism that the action categories were too complex to be applied in practice.

A further set of draft Regulations was published at the end of 1988. If implemented, they would have required employers to make an assessment of their manual handling operations and to take all necessary steps to prevent reasonably foreseeable injury to employees from the handling of loads at work. However, it was then found that discussions were proceeding at two levels – in the UK and the EC, so it was decided that the UK discussions should be suspended and efforts concentrated on getting the European Directive on Manual Handling right, which have now established the framework for all EC Member States – including the UK.

The main requirements of UK legislation are likely to be:

- a duty on the employer to take the appropriate organisational measures, or use the appropriate means (such as mechanical equipment) to avoid the need for manual handling of loads by workers;
- a duty on the employer to take action to reduce the risk where manual handling cannot be avoided. This will involve carrying out an assessment, not only of the lifting activity, but also of the workplace itself;
- a duty on the employer to provide proper information, instruction and training, and to consult with workers and/or their representatives.

Visual display units

Over the past 10 years, VDUs have gone from being a rarity in offices to being on the majority of desks. Such a rapid development has been associated with a number of fears, concerning in particular:

- the effects on the neck, arms and hands of sitting at a keyboard typing for long periods;
- the effects on the eyes of looking at a VDU screen for long periods;
- the possible effects of electromagnetic fields on pregnant women.

Large-scale studies have shown that the first two of these are controllable by ergonomic means – i.e. using the right equipment, properly adjusted. The risk to pregnant women remains unproven. Proposed EC legislation includes:

- a requirement that all VDU users be provided with the correct furniture, given the nature and frequency of their VDU usage, and instruction in how to adjust it properly;
- a duty to provide appropriate lighting;
- a duty to arrange eyesight testing on first starting work with VDUs, and at other times if there is evidence of a problem;

Enforcement

The Health and Safety at Work Act rationalised and broadened the requirements placed on employers regarding health and safety issues. At the same time, the arrangements for enforcement were simplified and extended, the main changes being: the bringing together of the existing central government safety inspectorates under new arrangements based on a policy body (the Health and Safety Commission – HSC) and an executive arm (the Health and Safety Executive – HSE); and the creation of new enforcement powers for inspectors, notably the power to issue Prohibition Notices and Improvement Notices.

In practice, most UK employers will be subject to inspection either by the Health and Safety Executive or by the local authority (e.g. district or borough council). Who does what is determined by the Health and Safety (Enforcing Authority) Regulations 1989, but as a rule of thumb, the HSE is responsible for industrial premises, while commercial premises such as shops, offices and hotels are covered by local authorities.

Two further principles are that there should be no dual inspection (two authorities responsible for the same activity) nor self inspection (an authority inspecting its own offices!). So, while offices are generally inspected by local authorities, an office within a factory or an airport would come under the HSE. The principle of no self inspection means that the HSE's offices are inspected by the relevant local authority and vice versa. This may seem a legal nicety but in practice it is important for personnel managers to know which authority deals with their premises.

Not only do notifications have to be made to the enforcing authority (e.g. accidents and certain cases of ill health resulting from work), but employees are entitled to know which enforcing authority they come under (Health and Safety Information for Employees Regulations 1989). The Act gives inspectors (HSE and local authority) a number of powers to enable them to implement the Act. These can be divided into information-gathering and enforcement powers.

In order to collect the information they need, inspectors have a right to enter and inspect places where people work. They can interview and take statements from people, they can take photographs and measurements, and they can take samples – e.g. of dust in the atmosphere, or of materials used in the process.

The HSE's policy is to work by co-operation with the organisations it inspects, but where the advice of its inspectors is ignored, or there is a serious failure to control risk, inspectors can use a variety of enforcement powers. Where there is an imminent risk of serious personal injury (e.g. handling a highly corrosive or toxic material without adequate precautions to ensure people's health) the inspector can serve a Prohibition Notice to stop work altogether until things are put right.

In situations where there is no imminent and serious risk, but there is nevertheless a breach of some relevant legal requirement, the inspector can serve an Improvement Notice. This allows work to continue but requires remedial action within a specified period. The period has to be at least 21 days and is normally discussed with the managers involved before the Notice is served. An example of a situation where an Improvement Notice might be served is where there are moderate to high noise levels and no proper arrangements for assessment and control have been made under the Noise at Work Regulations 1989.

Anyone who has an Improvement or Prohibition Notice served on them has the right to appeal against it to an Industrial Tribunal, who then have powers to either cancel, amend or uphold it. Whether a Notice has been served or not, inspectors have the power to take criminal proceedings against anyone on whom duties are placed by the Act. This could therefore include companies, other employers, as well as individual directors, managers and employees. As in any other criminal case, the onus is on the prosecutor, the inspector, to prove the case beyond a reasonable doubt.

This has caused problems in the past in health-related cases. It has sometimes been difficult for inspectors to get evidence to prove a risk to health, especially with materials such as asbestos, where illness may appear only many years after exposure to the substance.

It has been argued that COSHH and other post-1974 legislation make it easier for inspectors to prosecute over health issues. For example, where no health risk assessment has been carried out as required by COSHH, that would be an offence in itself regardless of whether any individual employee had actually suffered damage to health – and much easier for the inspector to prove.

If the case succeeds, the maximum penalty will depend on which court imposes sentence. In the magistrates' court, the maximum penalty is a fine of £2000 per offence, although increases are planned. In the Crown court, there is no limit on the fine. In some cases, a prison sentence of up to two years can be imposed either instead of, or as well as, a fine.

Civil cases

So far we have concentrated on inspectors' enforcement of the Act through the criminal courts. However, where an employee's health is damaged because of the work he or she does, there is another form of legal action which may well in practice involve a far higher financial penalty for an organisation and its insurers – the injured employee's 'civil claim'.

To sue the employer successfully, the employee has to prove that he/she has suffered loss (e.g. loss of earnings), that this loss resulted from an event which took place at work, and that this event was the result of either negligence or breach of statutory duty by his or her employer.

Negligence

The first stage in a negligence case is for the person seeking compensation (the plaintiff) to prove that the person being sued had a 'duty of care' to him or to her. This is a technicality in claims made by employees against their employers, since it has long been established in case law that all employers have a duty of care to their employees.

Secondly, the plaintiff has to prove that the employer was negligent – that is, failed to take reasonable care for his or her health and safety.

Note that under the principle of vicarious liability, each employer can be held responsible for the negligent actions of all its employees while they are 'in the course of their employment', so the fact that the injury resulted from the negligence of the plaintiff's fellow employee would not be a defence.

Breach of statutory duty

Where employees are protected by specific health and safety legislation, they may be able to claim damages for 'breach of statutory duty'. This is saying in effect that the injury resulted from the employer's failure to comply with the specific legislation in force for the employee's protection.

Employees often claim both negligence and breach of statutory duty – the so called 'double-barrelled action'. This is not surprising since the same set of circumstances – e.g. defective extract ventilation causing employees to be exposed to hazardous fumes – may well amount to both negligence (failure to take reasonable care) and a failure to comply with relevant legislation.

Since COSHH and other post-1974 legislation such as the Noise at Work Regulations extend the specific statutory duties placed on organisations to protect their employees, it may well now prove easier for an employee to claim compensation for breach of statutory duty – e.g. following ill health caused by the person's work.

However, as many work-related illnesses have a long latent period (i.e. the time between exposure to a harmful substance and resulting ill health being diagnosed), and as what the courts consider is the law and state of technical knowledge at the time the damage (e.g. over-exposure) is alleged to have occurred, it will take many years for a significant body of case law to be built up.

A further problem for employees seeking compensation is that the onus is on them to prove the link between the working conditions/environment and the disease, illness or other ill health in respect of which they are claiming compensation.

This cause and effect link is usually much harder to prove in a health case as opposed to a safety case, as the factors influencing health are simultaneously more complex and less well understood than those involved in traditional industrial safety.

Influence of the EC

An essential principle underlying the Single European Market is that employers throughout the EC should work to common standards of, among other things, health and safety at work.

Comparisons between EC Member States have suggested that there are currently major differences, both in terms of standards (e.g. health and safety at work legislation) and enforcement of those standards.

Work has been proceeding for some time now on 'harmonising' standards, and it was in 1988 that the European Commission

1. **Safety and Ergonomics at Work**
   - completion of the internal market and the removal of technical barriers;
   - promotion of safety at work and the application of ergonomic principles;
   - safety in high-risk sectors (sea, agriculture, construction).
2. **Occupational Health and Hygiene**
   - occupational exposure limits for selected substances;
   - carcinogens;
   - measurement of occupational exposure;
   - proscription of certain substances;
   - noise;
   - dangerous preparations;
   - industrial diseases;
   - occupational health services.
3. **Information**
   - dissemination of information to workers on the consequences of technological change;
   - dissemination of information on specific chemical substances;
   - research on improvement of working conditions for employees;
   - exchange of information between national inspectorates.
4. **Training**
   - training in the workplace and for safety instructors;
   - training and recognition of those responsible for health and safety in the workplace;
   - health and safety for those participating in youth training schemes;
   - inclusion of health and safety training in the professional specialisations for those likely to be responsible for the health and safety of others (e.g. engineers and industrial chemists);
   - extension of Community training modules in high risk areas.
5. **Small and Medium-sized Enterprises**
   A Commission programme is envisaged to assess the impact of Community legislation on small and medium-sized enterprises and how information on implementing such legislation might best be communicated to such enterprises.
6. **Social Dialogue**
   The Advisory Committee (on Safety, Hygiene and Health Protection) will endeavour to foster a 'social dialogue' between employers and employees.

Figure 2.4 EC plan on safety, hygiene and health at work

published details of a six point programme, its most recent on the topic of safety, hygiene and health at work (see Figure 2.4).

The EC has already had a great influence on the health at work legislation that has been introduced in the last few years. COSHH, for example, is a vehicle for the implementation of a number of EC Directives, and the Noise at Work Regulations are almost word for word the same as EC Directive 86/188/EEC on the Protection of Workers from the Risks Related to Exposure to Noise at Work. Asbestos, safety signs and the packaging/labelling of dangerous goods are other topics on which the UK has had to bring in legislation to implement EC Directives.

This strong influence is likely to continue in the future, with the EC – rather than the UK Government – taking the lead in shaping the legal requirements on health in the workplace. The VDU and Manual Handling Directives have already been mentioned; both are examples of legislation that is likely to apply to a very large number of employers.

CHECKLIST

- Are we aware of the legal requirements relating to health as they apply to our workplace?
- Are there systems for taking whatever action is necessary to comply, and for monitoring the effectiveness of those systems?
- Do we have access to the appropriate technical expertise?
- Do we have suitable information systems so that we are informed of new and impending legislation in the health at work field – including that coming from the EC?
- Is there up-to-date information on any chemicals and other substances we use?
- Has there been an assessment of the potential hazards to health created by our operations, and has action been taken to eliminate or minimise those risks as appropriate?
- Do we keep the records required by law?
- Is there a system for people to report hazards, and for action to be taken to investigate and act on such reports?
- Do we have adequate insurance cover in respect of civil claims which might be made by employees?
- Is it our policy to go beyond the minimum standards required by the law to safeguard the health of our employees?

CHAPTER 3
Health Screening

Corporate health screening has progressed from being a senior executive 'perk', to an approach to safeguarding and enhancing the health of large groups of employees. To be effective, screening needs to address real healthcare priorities, and to be integrated with other corporate programmes such as health education.

Health screening tests should address diseases which are common in the group being screened, and responsive to action to treat or prevent the disease. A pressing example is risk factor assessment for coronary heart disease, which fulfils both sets of criteria.

Corporate health screening has been transformed by new technology, which enables a wide range of tests to be undertaken quickly and at low cost, within the workplace. Some screening can be undertaken by employers with suitable staff, but there is also a wide range of providers offering screening programmes for employees.

In the first chapter, we noted that the introduction of health screening into companies as a 'perk' for senior executives, has not always been a good thing; it has often created an elitist image for health screening. Some, though not all, trade unions have opposed the introduction of screening because of this image, and because it involves the purchase of services from the private medical sector. Such barriers are now breaking down. The benefits of providing specific screening services to entire workforces are being realised, and many such programmes are in operation. The providers of health screening to companies are by no means only the big private healthcare providers, and include many parts of the National Health Service.

Objectives

So what is health screening, and why should companies consider its introduction? Health screening has been defined as medical investigation which does not arise from a patient's request for advice for a specific complaint. There are three possible reasons for this activity:

1. To directly contribute to the health of individuals, by identifying the early signs of disease whilst effective action can still be taken.
2. To protect public health – for example, to assist the investigation of a food poisoning outbreak.
3. Research – for example, to check the effectiveness of a medical procedure before introducing it more widely.

It is the first of these reasons which will be considered in this chapter and, for the sake of clarity, it is worth saying a little more about just what the 'early signs of disease' might be. Firstly, they may be actual evidence of a disease in its early stages but not yet causing troublesome symptoms – a pre-cancerous growth, or slight deafness. Second, and very important in current screening programmes, the screening may look for 'risk factors'. These are not evidence of the existence of disease, but are factors which are known to be statistically linked to the occurrence of disease if unchecked. More will be said about risk factor screening later – an example is the detection of high levels of cholesterol in the blood. This is not a disease or a symptom in itself, but is known to be linked to the occurrence of coronary heart disease and therefore, presumably, worth trying to reduce.

For organisations then, health screening is a means of identifying signs of illness or potential illness amongst employees at a sufficiently early stage for effective treatment, correction, or avoidance to be undertaken. The benefits, to express them in somewhat Machiavellian terms, are that healthier, longer-lived employees work better and have less absence through illness. However, in compiling a benefits list, there are other factors which organisations might like to consider.

Health screening of groups of people produces a *level of interest in health* which goes beyond those factors which are the subject of the screening. Once motivated to take an interest in their health, many individuals become generally committed to looking after their bodies, to the benefit of themselves and their employers.

Once a group of people has been screened, their results can be *statistically analysed* to show health patterns and problems in the workplace. Such analysis need not breach the confidentiality of any individual result, but can show employers the priorities for action if overall health is to be further improved. In this way, health screening at work can be linked with other corporate health initiatives, such as health education.

Health screening is perceived by employees as a *major employment benefit* – almost certainly regarded as more valuable than the same amount of money awarded as a salary increment. Employee surveys have shown that healthcare provision is rated as one of the most important services which employers can provide.

Guidelines

How can a manager, responsible for the provision of employee benefits in, say, a medium-sized company, possibly review the huge range of employee screening options available and choose the most appropriate tests? This section will suggest some guidelines which the corporate buyer can use to assess relevance and value for money.

First, an important principle should be stated. This appears in most writing on the subject of health screening and is, in the words of a recent review by Holland and Steward that 'we must be sure that screening is not being used to identify conditions that are either untreatable or insignificant since at either end of this spectrum lie anguish and anxiety'. In other words, screening should be used to identify conditions where intervention is possible and worthwhile. There is no point in identifying something if no action can be taken as a result – and indeed some screening still provokes anxiety because of fear that the result will be bad news and that nothing can be done.

The academic literature on health screening sets out several other principles which have been used to assess the validity of screening programmes. These are no less relevant in an employment setting, and provide useful checklists in reviewing company programmes. Basic principles were set out for the World Health Organisation by Wilson and Jungner, and can be summarised as follows:

- the condition sought should be an important health problem;
- there should be an accepted treatment for individuals who are found to have the disease;
- facilities for diagnosis and treatment should be available;
- there should be a recognisable latent or early symptomatic stage;
- there should be a suitable test or examination;
- the test should be acceptable to the population being screened;
- the history of the disease, from its latent stage to being a declared disease, should be adequately understood;
- there should be an agreed policy on whom to treat as patients;

- the cost of the tests and the treatment should be economically balanced in relation to possible expenditure on medical care as a whole;
- the screening should be a continuing process and not a one-off project.

Another useful checklist was suggested by Cochrane and Holland for assessing any particular screening test. In this case seven criteria were identified:

1. Simplicity. A test should be simple to perform and the results easy to interpret. Where possible, the test should be capable of use by paramedical and other personnel.
2. Acceptability. Since participation in screening is voluntary, a test must be acceptable to those receiving it.
3. Accuracy. The test must give a true measurement of the condition under investigation.
4. Cost. The expense of the test must be considered in relation to the benefits of early detection of the disease.
5. Precision or repeatability. The test should give consistent results in repeated trials.
6. Sensitivity. The test should be capable of giving a positive finding when the person has the disease being sought.
7. Specificity. The test should be capable of giving a negative finding when the person does not have the disease being sought.

The guidelines provided above are important, and remind the company that when buying medical services, they will have to be compatible with medical ethical standards. This is not to suggest that the company will have to apply all of the listed criteria to every test being considered – you can reasonably expect the service provider to have done that – but there will undoubtedly be occasions when particular tests are requested and some guidelines will be required in order to come to a decision. It is also worth noting the scientific rigour behind the principles proposed. They are not based on sentiment or placebo value. In the words of Holland and Stewart, 'screening should be a hard-headed professional exercise rather than a form of evangelism'.

Application of the above guidelines will exclude many things which could technically be included in a company health screening programme, but will still leave a long list of options of legitimate screening tests. It is therefore worth taking a pragmatic look at the needs of organisations, and considering the issues which will influence the make-up of the final screening programme. Here we suggest four key

---

principles for consideration:

First, ensure that potential hazards in the workplace are taken into account in devising a health screening programme.

The individual health factors reviewed in this book are, of necessity, somewhat generalised. They assume 'average' populations. But there are many reasons why a particular workforce might not be average, and these include their workplace conditions. For example people handling toxic chemicals, exposed to noise, required to lift heavy weights, etc., will all have particular healthcare needs which should be anticipated in screening proposals. It is perhaps worth adding that identifying and controlling workplace hazards is likely to be a particular requirement for employers because it is their direct, probably legal, responsibility. Further guidance is given in Chapters 2 and 5, and in publications from the Health and Safety Executive.

Second, in any screening programme, include tests which evaluate ability to do the job without risks to safety and health.

Again, this is a reminder that all businesses are different and that a screening programme must be relevant to the specific needs of the organisation. Thus, while the workplace might not present any exceptional hazards, the employees might need some particular individual characteristics or attributes to do their job properly and safely. For example, vehicle driving requires good eyesight, fast reactions, and so on; food handling requires freedom from infectious organisms; manual handling requires strength and fitness. Before such tests are instituted, however, it is essential to prove that the test really does identify factors which could prevent the individual doing the job safely, especially if there is a risk of discriminating by gender or race.

Third, ensure the screening is suited to the particular characteristics of the workforce.

This is important because special health risks to a group of people might be created not by the working environment, but by the group itself. If the working group is non-typical, a 'standard' health screen may be inappropriate. Obvious examples are that tests specifically for women are not appropriate for an all male workforce, and vice versa. Age distribution too, is relevant in deciding the most appropriate tests for a particular population. Other factors include lifestyle characteristics of the workforce – it could be worth testing liver function in a high alcohol-consumption group – but here there is a Catch-22 dilemma: some health surveillance may be required before the full health surveillance requirements can be determined. In practice this is not such a problem – as the principles above noted, screening should be a continuing process, and results from previous programmes can be used to determine priorities for programmes that follow.

Finally, provide screening to the largest possible population, rather than undertaking extensive screening for a small population.

Comments have already been made about the 'executive medical' – a comprehensive examination provided to a small sector of the workforce, identified by their level of seniority. This is usually justified on the grounds that senior managers are expensive to replace when ill, but it is not necessarily a good use of a company's healthcare budget. If anything, executives are *less* prone to illness and absenteeism than other employees. Also, since health screening is subject to the law of diminishing returns, the best value for money will almost certainly be obtained by providing the most important tests for as many people as possible.

There are some other good reasons for spreading the benefit of health screening, and covering the largest possible workforce. One is difficult to appreciate until experienced, but is then very compelling. It is that an enthusiasm for health and fitness develops which continues well beyond the period of screening. Employees become competitive and monitor progress towards their targets – for weight, fitness, cholesterol reduction, etc. This is a very positive benefit in its own right, as well as achieving commitment to future health initiatives at work. Another extremely important benefit from screening large numbers was mentioned earlier. It is that the data can be analysed to show the overall health of the workforce, and the priorities for future action. In other words, healthcare resource can be precisely targeted to areas of maximum need – and the baseline will have been measured to show whether the health objectives were met.

Diseases

One of the earlier guidelines was that screening tests should address 'important health problems'. So what are the important health problems? An indication is given by Figure 3.1, which shows a breakdown of the leading causes of death in Great Britain. This is not the whole story of course – we are interested in illness, not just death – but the causes of death generally mirror the causes of suffering and absenteeism. Top of the cause of death table comes coronary heart disease,

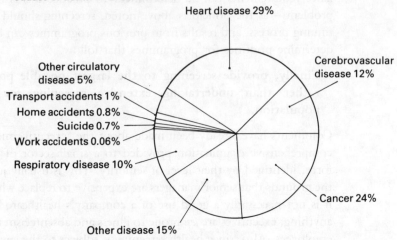

Causes of death in Great Britain

Heart disease 29%

Cerebrovascular disease 12%

Other circulatory disease 5%

Transport accidents 1%

Home accidents 0.8%

Suicide 0.7%

Work accidents 0.06%

Respiratory disease 10%

Cancer 24%

Other disease 15%

Figure 3.1 Causes of death in Great Britain

a once obscure disease, now the leading cause of death in Western society.

The next highest cause of death is cancer, but presenting cancer in this way, as though it was a single disease, is rather misleading. Cancer is really a term encompassing many different diseases, though a few are dominant. Lung cancer is the most common, accounting for a quarter of cancer deaths. Cancer of the large intestine and rectum (bowel cancer), and cancer of the breast each account for about 10 per cent of cancer deaths (though breast cancer is much the highest cause of cancer death if women are considered alone). There are then a range of other cancer sites, including the stomach, bladder, and skin. Continuing with the breakdown, the next major cause of death is cerebrovascular disease, or stroke. Next in the list is respiratory disease – again, really a number of diseases with pneumonia accounting for about half, and bronchitis about a quarter.

The above breakdown is interesting, and takes us part of the way to deciding the priorities for corporate health screening. However, a screening programme simply based on causes of death in Great Britain would blatantly disregard almost all of the principles which have been set out above! To devise a sensible screening programme we need, above all, to know which illnesses account for the most *premature* deaths, and which could be *prevented or cured*, if detected early.

In looking for the causes of premature deaths, a valuable source of information is the annual survey published by the Department of Health under the name 'On the State of the Public Health for the

Year'. Figure 3.2 is a table showing the main causes of death at different ages. This shows that for young people, the greatest risk of death results from road accidents. One out of every 50 young people is killed or seriously injured within 10 years of leaving school – with motor cyclists particularly at risk. In early middle age, the main causes of death are different for men and women. For men the major cause is heart disease, for women it is breast cancer. In the next age band, where mortality is sharply rising, heart disease is the leading cause of death for both men and women, as it is for the next age band, and for mortality taken overall.

The Department of Health statistics present the data in one other way, which is important in considering health priorities for workplace health programmes. This is to show how many years of working life are lost as a result of the major diseases. In other words, a cause of death which affected relatively young people would appear strongly in this analysis, while a cause which only affected people after their retirement age would not feature at all. This is thus a good indicator of the causes of premature death. The main data are summarised in Figure 3.3 and show, once again, coronary heart disease leading the league table. Most of the other causes are not surprising, given the figures already considered, and include motor accidents, respiratory disease, lung cancer, strokes, and breast cancer. However, the appearance of suicide in the list is a surprise. This arises because, although suicide is not one of the

Main causes of death at different ages · England, 1989
From Department of Health Report

Age 1-14	M	Road accidents	20%
	F	Congenital abnormalities	16%
Age 15-34	M	Road accidents	25%
	F	Road accidents	14%
Age 35-54	M	Heart disease	31%
	F	Cancer	22%
Age 55-74	M	Heart disease	35%
	F	Heart disease	24%
Age over 74	M	Heart disease	27%
	F	Heart disease	24%
All ages	M	Heart disease	30%
	F	Heart disease	23%

Figure 3.2   Main causes of death at different ages, England 1989

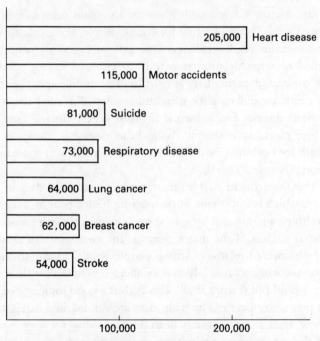

205,000	Heart disease
115,000	Motor accidents
81,000	Suicide
73,000	Respiratory disease
64,000	Lung cancer
62,000	Breast cancer
54,000	Stroke

100,000   200,000

Future years of working life lost

England and Wales 1988 from Department of Health Report

Figure 3.3   Major causes of lost working life

major causes of death in Great Britain (about 4,000 deaths per year are due to suicide), it particularly affects young people – especially males – and therefore contributes a high level of years of life lost.

It was suggested earlier that, to justify inclusion in a screening programme, the disease under consideration would need to meet one further condition. This is that it should be possible to prevent or cure the condition, given sufficient early knowledge. Let us consider the main causes of premature death again to review this requirement:

Coronary heart disease (CHD)

This is undoubtedly a candidate for very serious consideration, since only a small percentage reduction would represent a saving of many lives. CHD results in the deaths of some 180,000 people per year in the United Kingdom – 21 every hour. It accounts for 30 per cent of all deaths in men, and 25 per cent in women. Its enormous death toll is associated with an even higher level of illness and suffering, since the majority of heart attacks are not fatal. An enormous amount of

LOOKING AFTER CORPORATE HEALTH

research has gone into studying the causes of heart disease, and has established that the incidence of CHD is statistically linked with a number of so-called 'risk factors', many of which are aspects of personal lifestyle, such as cigarette smoking. This strongly suggests that CHD *could* be prevented, and that it is a priority not just for health screening, but for health education programmes. Screening for CHD risk factors will be considered in detail in the next section.

Cerebrovascular disease (stroke)

Like CHD, this condition is usually caused by obstruction of the arteries. In CHD the arteries supplying blood to the heart muscle are blocked; in a stroke, the same process blocks the blood supply to the brain. About 100,000 people in Great Britain suffer a stroke each year, and about 25,000 people die. Since the process of artery obstruction is so similar to that in CHD, the disease is related to the same risk factors (though not with exactly the same statistical distribution), and is another priority for screening and health education.

Motor accidents

Motor accidents appear as the second highest cause of lost years of working life. Since they rank relatively low in the overall cause of death table (about 5000 deaths per year), it is clear that many of the victims are young people. Indeed, road accidents are much the most common cause of death in the 5 to 24 years age group, accounting for over two thirds of all deaths in this group. The cost of road accidents to society is extremely high, estimated at more than £3 billion per year, and represents one of the pressing challenges to public health. This is unquestionably relevant to employers, who lose significant productive resource from road deaths and injuries, but can screening programmes make any contribution? The answer is that there is probably some part to play – through eyesight testing for instance – but that this is probably more a candidate for training and education, to be tackled in Chapter 10.

Respiratory disease

As has been mentioned before, this is actually a number of conditions. However, collectively they represent the third most important cause of death in most developed countries (after heart disease and cancer). Unless the respiratory disease is likely to have an occupational cause (as may be the case for those who work with dusts and chemicals), then preventive health screening is likely to be of limited value. Most respiratory diseases are detected and treated by their symptoms, and pre-symptomatic detection appears to offer little to improve overall quality or length of life. Despite this, lung function testing, or spirometry, is often included in employment health screens. This may often give helpful reassurance when all is well, but is probably not a screening priority. One point which should be mentioned at this stage is that some respiratory diseases are caused, and all are aggravated, by cigarette smoking. This will be considered in more detail in Chapter 8, but does have some significance in health screening considerations since many screening tests draw attention to problems associated with smoking.

Lung cancer

This disease accounts for about 40,000 deaths per year in Great Britain, the highest rate in the world. The death rate amongst men is about twice that in women, although the last 30 years have seen a declining rate in men and an increasing rate in women. It is sometimes thought that the chest x-ray is a screening test for lung cancer. However, if a lung tumour is detected on a chest x-ray, the prospect of effective treatment is poor, and the test could not be justified for that purpose. Regular chest x-rays were introduced primarily to detect and control tuberculosis. They involve unnecessary exposure to radiation, albeit small, and now serve little purpose as a routine screen unless there are workplace environmental hazards which require health surveillance (for example asbestos), or unless there are relevant symptoms. As with respiratory disease, a more productive approach is to tackle the cause of 90 per cent of lung cancer – cigarette smoking.

Breast cancer

Mortality for this disease has been slowly increasing for most of this century with current rates at about 14,000 deaths per year. About one third of these deaths are among women under 65. For comparison with other illness statistics, the figures for women only should be used – for instance, for women breast cancer is a more important cause of death than lung cancer. Although the causes of breast cancer are not yet known, there is good reason to believe that environmental and social factors are important. British women are four times more likely than Japanese women to develop breast cancer, but when Japanese women emigrate to the west, the breast cancer rate in their children rises to western levels. A number of factors are known to have a statistical link with the disease. They include early date of first period, and late first pregnancy. These are not useful observations in a screening context, and therefore the most useful approach to limiting the death rate is early detection.

Screening to detect breast cancer is based on specialist x-ray techniques known as mammography, combined with clinical examination of the breasts. Following an extensive study of the evidence for screening, a DHSS committee chaired by Sir Patrick Forrest recommended a national programme in which women aged 50–64 should be screened every three years. It was estimated that mammography can reduce mortality by one-third or more, by detecting cancer sufficiently early to allow effective treatment. The Forrest report was accepted by the government, and was expected to save 2,000 lives per year among women over 50. Some work is still to be done on the risk associated with the radiation from mammography, but this is likely to be small in comparison with its benefits.

Screening tests

This chapter has so far looked at some principles which can be used to assess screening tests, and some of the diseases which particularly affect working men and women. It is now time to consider some actual screening tests which can be included in corporate healthcare programmes. Given that health screening should address health issues which are both common and treatable, one candidate stands out strongly. It is **coronary heart disease**.

The staggering figures for the incidence of coronary heart disease (CHD) have already been discussed. It was also noted that CHD is statistically linked with a number of factors, some of which can be controlled. These are the main 'risk factors' for CHD:

- age;
- blood cholesterol level;
- high blood pressure;
- cigarette smoking;
- diabetes;
- family history;
- lack of exercise;
- obesity;
- sex (male);
- stress.

There has been some criticism that the term 'risk factor' is misleading because it implies that these actually *cause* the risk of CHD. This is not necessarily the case – the risk factor may merely have a role in some complex process which results in CHD. In some cases the importance of one risk factor may be that it is the cause of another risk factor – for instance, stress may cause high blood pressure. However, for now their importance is that many of the risk factors can be identified by health screening, and that reducing risk factors should lower the risk of heart disease.

Including the above risk factors in a health screen is relatively straightforward – some are self-evident, others simply involve asking questions in a way which is likely to obtain an honest response. But two relatively recent developments have greatly enhanced the power and usefulness of screening for CHD risk factors in the workplace environment. The first is the introduction of the 'desk top' blood analyser. These are instruments, about the size of a typewriter, which measure a component of blood using only a small drop – usually obtained by pricking a finger. The blood analysis is produced in only a few minutes. After some teething troubles, which resulted in inaccuracy, these instruments are now reliable and give good precision in the hands of skilled operators. They are ideal for measuring blood cholesterol levels, when the advantage of providing and explaining the results at the time of the screening is enormous.

The second notable development is the use of computers in CHD screening. These make it possible to calculate quickly the significance of several risk factors in combination. Figure 3.4 shows the cumulative effect of three factors, and demonstrates that such combinations can be extremely important in predicting true CHD risk. Much of the data used to assess CHD risk is derived from a major study in the town of Framingham, Massachusetts USA, but handling the volume of data involved would not be realistic during a routine health screen – without a computer. Programs now exist which take individual screening results, and compute the resultant risk of CHD. This is extremely motivating to an individual considering making lifestyle changes to improve health. Just as importantly, it shows exactly what lifestyle changes would produce the greatest benefit, and can set targets for improvements.

It is sometimes thought that CHD screening is primarily a 'male' screen, while screening for women should concentrate on breast and cervical cancer. It is therefore important to emphasise that coronary risk factors are a real priority for women too. It is certainly the case that men are more at risk from CHD than women – which is why sex is in the list of risk factors. But this is still a major health issue for women, causing 25 per cent of all deaths (compared with 5 per cent for breast cancer).

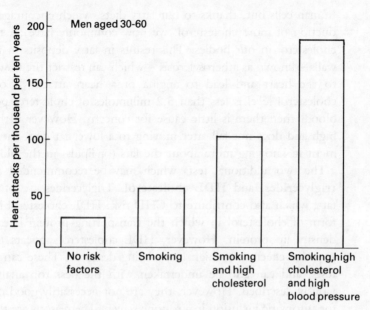

Figure 3.4 Effect of combining risk factors

A look at the list of risk factors will show another advantage of preventive heart disease screening. It is that most of the factors are also associated with other important diseases. Virtually all are relevant in reducing the risk of strokes. Cigarette smoking is the cause of most lung cancer, and features strongly in respiratory diseases. High blood pressure increases the risk of kidney disease and leg vessel disease. Equally important, when individuals are shown the health risks associated with their particular results, this does not have to be presented as 'bad news'; indeed, very much the opposite is the case. Armed with a clear understanding of their risks, and some attainable targets for improvement, most individuals can make real improvements to their health risks.

Blood tests

While considering screening for heart disease, we should say a little more about **blood tests**. It has already been noted that the level of cholesterol in the blood is an important CHD risk factor, and that cholesterol measurement is now straightforward with results produced in just a few minutes. Cholesterol is a white, waxy substance produced in the liver. It is transported in the blood attached to a protein known as low density lipoprotein (LDL). Cholesterol is a vital component of human cells but, thanks to our fatty diets, which encourage the production of more cholesterol, we now commonly have far too much cholesterol in our bodies. This results in fatty deposits in the artery walls – known as atherosclerosis – which can restrict the flow of blood to the heart and lead to angina or a heart attack. If our blood cholesterol level is less than 5.2 millimoles of cholesterol per litre of blood, then there is little cause for concern. However if the level is high and does not fall after moving to a lower fat diet, then there is merit in knowing more about the fats (or lipids) in the blood.

The two additional tests which may be recommended are blood **triglycerides**, and **HDL cholesterol**. Triglycerides are other blood fats, which also contribute to CHD risk. HDL cholesterol is another form of cholesterol in which the transporting protein is called high density lipoprotein. However, HDL cholesterol appears to have a *protective* effect, with high levels being desirable. These can be useful tests, and can also be undertaken with the desk-top analysers previously described. However, they are not necessarily good candidates for automatic inclusion in a routine screen. The reasons are that firstly, if the total cholesterol level is low then knowing more about other blood lipids is simply not a priority. Secondly, the additional tests must be carried out on fasting blood to give accurate results. In other words, the individual must go through the inconvenience of not eating for ten to twelve hours – probably for no additional benefit.

Exercise stress test

Another test which is often discussed when heart disease screening is being considered is the **exercise stress test**. This is a complex test in which the individual's ECG (electrocardiogram) is monitored during controlled exercise on a treadmill or bicycle. While a resting ECG is of little value as a screening test, since it may be quite normal even in high-risk individuals, the exercise ECG is much more likely to reveal evidence of heart disease. However, aside from the high cost of this test, which may rule it out of most corporate health screening programmes, there are other drawbacks. These relate to the occurrence of false negative and false positive results. A false negative result of a screening test is a result which suggests all is well when there are actually problems. A false positive result suggests there are problems when there are not. All screening tests produce some false results – it is just a fact of life that nothing is 100 per cent certain. However, as some calculations by Dr Stephen Campbell show, false results can be a particular problem with exercise ECGs.

Dr Campbell suggested that a 40-year-old male with no obvious heart risk factors would have only a 23 per cent likelihood of heart disease if he had a positive result from an exercise test. Thus, while a negative result could be extremely reassuring, 77 per cent of such men with a positive result would be subject to unnecessary anxiety and further testing. On the other hand, when this approach is applied to someone with a higher general probability of heart disease – a 50-year-old male with perhaps one risk factor – then a positive result would be correct in about 88 per cent of cases, making it far more valuable. At the other end of the spectrum – say a 60-year-old male with many risk factors – a positive result will merely confirm what was already extremely likely, and the danger becomes that of a negative result being misleading, since there would still be a 92 per cent probability of heart disease. The exercise stress test, then, can probably be ruled out as a blanket screen to be applied to absolutely everyone, but this should not be taken to exclude its very powerful value for appropriate individuals, those who already show some likelihood of coronary heart disease.

Well woman screening

Moving on from heart disease, it is appropriate to look at an extremely popular approach to screening – **well woman screening**. Well woman screening consists of a combination of tests which seek to identify female specific cancers at a sufficiently early stage to allow effective treatment. **Mammography** (breast x-ray) has already been considered, and most experts agree that research evidence of its value is strong. Evidence also supports the inclusion of breast examination alongside mammography, and instruction of women in the techniques of breast self-examination.

Having considered the problems of false negatives and false positives in exercise stress testing, it is worth looking at the figures for breast cancer screening. The incidence of false negatives is about 20 per cent – in other words two out of ten women who have breast cancer will be told they have not. The false positive rate is about 10 per cent – one in ten people who do not have breast cancer will be told there may be an abnormality, and will have to go through further tests, and consequent anxiety, before getting the all clear. It should be stressed that, despite the value of mammography, it is not an appropriate routine screening test for young women. Opinions differ on the best age to start screening, and there is little evidence to date on the value of screening women younger than 50. This is primarily because breast cancer is mainly a disease of older women. However, some authorities advocate that screening should be introduced between ages 35 to 40, and most screening organisations adopt this advice on the grounds that 20 per cent of breast cancer arises in women younger than 50, and that they should not be denied the opportunity for early diagnosis and treatment.

The other main component of well woman screening programmes is the **cervical smear test**. This addresses a much less common form of cancer – cervical cancer causes about 2000 deaths per year – but is an extremely important test because it could virtually eliminate the disease. Cervical cancer affects the cervix – the neck of the womb. It is linked with sexual activity (early sexual intercourse and with multiple partners) – though by no means confined to those who are promiscuous. The cervical smear test is based on the fact that there are changes to cells on the surface of the cervix *before* they become cancerous. The smear is taken using a spatula or brush to scrape cells from the cervix, which are then sent to a laboratory for microscopic examination. If abnormalities are found early, then effective treatment can invariably be provided. Current national policy is to provide smear tests for all women aged between 20 and 64 at least every five years. Many experts argue that testing should be more frequent – at least every three years and ideally annually – though current NHS capacity means that annual screening could only be undertaken through private and employment based programmes.

Well woman screening is not necessarily confined to the tests described above, and the screening opportunity may be used to check blood pressure, to measure other coronary risk factors, to provide advice and counselling, and perhaps to undertake other specialist tests. In comparing well woman screens for price, convenience, etc., it is important to fully check the content.

Fitness testing

Another approach to screening which results in a 'package' of tests, is **fitness testing**. Health and fitness are different, though related, characteristics of the body. In essence, health is related to freedom from disease (though many definitions go well beyond this), while fitness is a measure of the body's ability to deliver work. There is currently an enormous renewal of interest in personal fitness, and many components of physical fitness can be measured. Fitness testing includes evaluation of strength, stamina, and suppleness, and will usually involve measurements taken during carefully controlled exercise. Measurements can include heart rate, blood pressure, and lung function. Computers are often used to process the results, and the report may include a personal graded exercise programme to encourage the individual to progress safely to a higher level of fitness. Fitness testing is often a very appropriate part of corporate healthcare programmes. It appeals to people with an interest in their health and, in most organisations, the fitness of employees is strongly related to their ability to do their work well.

The combination health screening programmes described so far illustrate the way in which much corporate screening is undertaken, and highlight some health screening priorities for the majority of employed people. However, there are a number of additional tests which can be valuable – either alone, or as additions to a broader programme. The following notes describe some of the most common tests included in corporate health screens.

Hearing tests

Hearing tests have limited value as routine screens in a normal population, but are important if the individuals are exposed to noise which might be damaging their hearing. If this is the case, hearing tests – or audiometry – can detect hearing loss before it becomes a handicap, and allow action to be taken to prevent further loss. It is also useful to follow the hearing of a group of people exposed to noise to ensure that the controls are sufficient to prevent noise-induced hearing loss. Audiometry involves exposing each ear to pure tone sound to find the lowest level which can just be heard. The result is known as an audiogram and shows hearing sensitivity at different frequencies. If audiometry has to be undertaken in a noisy workplace, then it will probably be necessary to install a soundproof booth in which to undertake the tests.

Vision tests

Vision tests are a valuable addition to company health programmes, especially if the employees need good eyesight to do their work, or might experience strain if they work without having good eyesight – as is the case for users of visual display units. Basic testing is relatively quick and straightforward, but it should be made clear that eyesight screening tests are not a substitute for full testing by an optician as a basis for prescribing spectacles – this will still be required if the vision test indicates any defects.

Stress tests

Stress testing is a relatively recent introduction into screening programmes, and involves the individual answering a series of questions which are known to be relevant to those suffering stress. The questions will usually be seeking to assess the personality type of the individual, the effect of recent stressful events, and any evidence of stress-related symptoms. In some cases these questions have very effectively been transferred to computer. Many individuals are happier giving the answers to personal questions to a computer, and the computer provides an instant analysis of results. Stress is a subject of much interest at the present time, and is dealt with in detail in Chapter 6. It must be emphasised that basic stress screening is not in any way a substitute for professional stress counselling – but may be valuable as a means of identifying those in need of further help.

Blood pressure measurement

Blood pressure measurement is quickly and easily performed by a trained nurse. Hypertension (high blood pressure) is usually easy to treat, and is a risk factor for many diseases including kidney failure and strokes. Most experts advise that blood pressure be measured annually from age 40, and younger if there is a history of hypertension in the family.

Occult blood tests

Occult blood tests have nothing to do with the supernatural – occult means hidden, and these tests look for the presence of blood in stool samples. The purpose is the identification of bowel cancer, the cause of nearly 20,000 deaths per year. The test involves either the collection of stool samples which are sent for analysis, or the provision of a test kit to the individual. This involves dropping an impregnated paper into the toilet after a bowel movement, and observing any colour change.

The problem with the test, aside from its unpleasantness, is the high level of false positives. There are many reasons for the presence of blood in stools, and only about 20 per cent of people with positive results will actually have cancer – the rest will unnecessarily have to suffer the extensive examinations needed to establish a diagnosis. There will also be a high level of false negatives, with up to 30 per cent of cancers being missed. At the present time, most experts seem to feel the value of stool testing is limited, and is certainly not justified for people aged under 50. However, bowel cancer is the second highest cause of cancer deaths, and further results from major screening trials are awaited with interest. If the accuracy of the test was to be improved, it could become an extremely important screen.

Urine tests

Urine tests for diabetes are an extremely cheap and effective way of screening for this potentially disabling condition. They are straightforward to include in a health screen and involve placing an impregnated dipstick in a urine sample, which then indicates the presence or otherwise of glucose. It is also useful to test for blood and for protein, which might give early indications of kidney disease. In view of the usefulness, simplicity, and cheapness of urine tests, they can be expected to be a feature of most routine health screening.

AIDS tests

AIDS testing should perhaps be considered here because it is a subject of interest to many employers, and questions are frequently asked about the inclusion of AIDS testing in health screens. AIDS does not yet meet the criterion used for assessing the seriousness of disease. The annual death rate is measured in hundreds rather than tens of thousands. However, its potential for being extremely serious is enormous, and it is the cause of much interest and anxiety. Testing is certainly possible – the usual test being for antibodies to the AIDS virus, HIV. However, no testing should be undertaken without all individuals giving their clear consent, and being counselled in detail about the possible consequences of a positive test result. The fact is that an HIV-positive individual does not present a risk to other employees in the vast majority of employment situations. There is therefore little benefit in undertaking AIDS testing for employee groups. A more productive approach to the threat of AIDS is health education, to be considered in Chapter 10, since AIDS is largely a preventable disease.

Blood tests

Blood tests have already been considered in the context of heart disease screening, where tests for blood lipids were described. However, many other components of blood can be analysed – often using the desk top analyser, with its advantage of immediate results. In addition to the test for blood fats such as cholesterol, other common blood tests include glucose for diabetes, uric acid for gout, gamma-glutamyltransferase (GGT) for liver damage, urea for renal disease, bilirubin for jaundice and haemoglobin for anaemia.

Blood tests can also be performed for drugs, including illicit drugs, as well as legal drugs used inappropriately. As for AIDS the likelihood of finding someone positive is generally low in the UK, and may create more questions than it answers. There are a few circumstances in which drug abuse can cause serious risks to others, but drug screening should only be introduced following discussion with employee representatives.

Health screening providers

It will probably not have escaped the reader of this book that there are many providers of health screening services! They tend to fall into four main categories:

1. Individual doctors who devote part of their practice to screening, either at their premises, or by visiting the client.
2. Large private medical groups who offer health screening as one of a range of services. Screening is often undertaken at their private hospital facilities.
3. Specialist screening companies who provide health screening and nothing else, either at screening centres or on a mobile basis.
4. Occupational health organisations who provide screening together with other corporate health services such as health education, first aid, etc.

All of these categories of provider are capable of providing excellent health screening services to organisations. However, it is worth talking to several before making a final decision, and the following questions should be considered in evaluating alternative providers:

- Do their health screening programmes meet the real needs and interests of your employees?
- Do they have an understanding of your business, and any legal or occupation-specific requirements you have?
- Do they have competent medical, technical, and occupational health advisers?
- Are the doctors and nurses who undertake the screening properly trained in screening and counselling techniques?
- Is there an adequate quality control programme to ensure accuracy of results?
- How are results presented to the individual – is there good feedback at the time of the screen, and in the form of well-written printed reports?
- Will they provide good reports to the organisation, with statistical analysis of results, and recommendations for future action?
- Are they able to provide follow-up services of additional tests, environmental monitoring, employee training, etc?
- Do they offer value for money, and do they compare well with their competitors?
- Are they always pleasant to deal with, and do they answer your enquiries efficiently?

Before leaving the subject of providers, we should mention two alternative providers. They are the National Health Service, and the organisation itself. There is sometimes resistance to providing for employees, tests which they could obtain from the NHS. Indeed one worthwhile action in a corporate healthcare programme would be to encourage employees to take up NHS screening options. However, the fact is that occupationally based screens achieve far higher take up rates than state screening services, and that the NHS simply does not have the resource to provide comprehensive screening packages with high quality reports, follow-up action programmes, and analysis of data for employee groups. If the screening has to include occupational-specific tests, then there is probably no option but to look to the private sector.

For an organisation to undertake its own health screening, there is one key requirement – competent staff. If the company employs its own doctor or nurse, then there is enormous opportunity to provide in-house screening. As has been mentioned, the area of health screening has been transformed by new, mobile screening technology, and by versatile screening computer programs. These are available to company doctors and nurses and enable powerful screens to be provided as an in-house service.

Introducing a screening programme

Health screening is invariably welcomed by employees, as a valuable employment benefit, and an important opportunity to take a serious interest in their own health. Perhaps the main consideration for employers introducing health screening is therefore to make the *most* of the exercise. There are two key principles involved in achieving this. First, the full commitment of the whole organisation should be evident. There is nothing quite as useful as the Chief Executive going for his or her screen, and then being seen to act on the results. The same goes for all managers and supervisors, where leadership by example will motivate the whole workforce. The second principle is that the health screening should be a *part* of the corporate healthcare programme. Improving the health of organisations requires action on several fronts, including environmental improvements, education, publicity, etc. A good screening provider will provide an analysis of results which will be invaluable in accurately establishing the priorities for additional actions.

One particular question to be resolved in introducing a health screening programme is whether to provide it on-site or off-site. Off-site screening has some obvious advantages. The screening can be undertaken in tailor-made facilities, with all services to hand, and with a degree of comfort which could not be provided in the average workplace. However, there are drawbacks too – the main one being the travelling time involved. Unless you happen to be situated extremely close to a screening centre, it is quite likely that the main cost of an extensive screening programme will turn out to be the time lost through employees being away from work. This is resolved by providing the screening on-site, in a suitable room in the workplace. It is surprising how effective this can be, and how an office can be transformed into a clinic when it has been set up with medical equipment. Some equipment, of course, cannot realistically be temporarily installed in a workplace – particularly x-ray equipment used for tests such as mammography. However, in this case it is possible to use a mobile service with the equipment installed in a vehicle which is parked close to the worksite for the duration of the screening programme.

Finally, how often should screening be undertaken? There is unfortunately no simple answer to this question. Frequency really has to depend upon the test itself, and the individual being tested. Sometimes it is best to start on a one-off basis, and then repeat the exercise depending on the results found and the interest generated. Alternatively, a good compromise is often to provide annual screening, but to omit some tests for low-risk individuals (such as those under 40, or those who had no significant risk factors in previous screening). If possible, it is also desirable to organise some tests on a *more* frequent basis. For example, it is frustrating for an employee to be given a target for a reduced cholesterol level, but not to know whether it has been achieved until a year has passed. Providing certain tests on, say, a quarterly follow-up basis will overcome this.

The following checklist is intended to clarify thinking about corporate health screening programmes, and to raise issues which may need investigation before a programme is introduced:

- What is the objective of our screening exercise? For example, is there some particular health concern to be addressed, or is the aim to provide an attractive perk?
- Who is to be screened? Can we provide the service for everyone, or is it limited? If limited, are those screened to be selected by seniority, age, sex, length of service, nature of work, or evidence of health risks?
- Is the screening to be undertaken off-site or at the workplace?
- What is the budget?
- What is the screen content to be? Does it definitely tackle priorities, and make good use of the budget?
- Who is our provider? Have they been carefully selected for quality and value for money?
- How is the screening to be integrated with other workplace health initiatives, such as health education?
- What is the planned frequency of screening?
- How will we follow-up high-risk individuals?
- How will we monitor the effectiveness of the service, and how will the overall analysis of screening results be acted upon?

CHAPTER 4
Acute Healthcare

All employers are required by law to make basic provision to treat employees who fall ill or suffer injury while at work. The scope of this provision will depend on the organisation itself, and in particular on the number of employees and the potential hazards involved in the work. However, many employers provide a treatment service which goes beyond the minimum first aid arrangements required by law.

Another key aspect – and one which is currently very topical – is the range of options which face the employer who wishes to fund the hospital care of employees, often through the provision of a private medical insurance plan.

Finally the importance of 'disaster planning' is emphasised – along with the need to ensure that health emergencies are considered within this planning process – and the essential principles of effective emergency plans are highlighted.

First aid

All employers have a legal obligation to be able to give first aid to their employees who are injured (or fall ill) at work. However, the extent of first aid provision will depend on the circumstances and several factors need to be taken into account. Clearly the number of employees is important, but the potential hazards of the work involved and the accessibility of hospital accident and emergency facilities must also be considered.

The legal responsibilities are laid down in the Health and Safety (First Aid) Regulations 1981 and as these are made under the Health and Safety at Work Act 1974 – and hence apply to almost every workplace in the UK – it is worth analysing them in some detail.

What is first aid?

For the purposes of the Regulations, first aid means two things. The first is:

'in cases where a person will need help from a medical practitioner or nurse, treatment for the purposes of preserving life and minimising the consequences of injury and illness until such help is obtained'.

On a superficial reading this seems a relatively minor role – a holding of the fort until the real experts arrive. However, experience shows that the time before the ambulance arrives is crucial.

A number of doctors have stressed the importance of the action taken in the first few minutes after injury or sudden illness strikes. Not only does it influence the effectiveness of treatment the individual receives later from a doctor or nurse, it can be a matter of life or death. This is illustrated by the case reported a few years ago where a worker in a meat factory accidentally stabbed himself in the groin with the knife he was using, severing one of the femoral arteries. He bled to death because no one knew how to staunch the bleeding.

The second key aspect of first aid identified by the Regulations is:

'treatment of minor injuries which would otherwise receive no treatment or which do not need treatment by a medical practitioner or nurse'.

This is self-explanatory, but one point worth noting is that while the first section quoted above refers to injury and illness, this one only mentions injury. It is therefore not part of first aid to give treatment for minor illnesses and ailments. In particular, first aiders should not be dispensing pain killers, even if these are products such as paracetamol which are classified as OTC (over the counter) medicines and which anyone can buy without a prescription. This question is dealt with in greater detail below, but here it is important to emphasise that dispensing such medicines does not form any part of first aid.

The Regulations go on to say that the employer must provide (or ensure there are provided) two things to enable first aid to be given to employees if they are injured or become ill while at work: first aid equipment/facilities and 'suitable persons'.

Both these requirements are qualified by the words 'adequate and appropriate in the circumstances'. This implies that the employer must make an assessment to determine what is 'adequate and appropriate', taking into account such factors as:

- the number of employees – clearly, the more employees there are, the greater the likelihood of someone needing first aid as defined;
- the work that is done – again, this will influence the likelihood of injuries (and possibly illnesses) occurring;
- the location of the workplace – in particular, how close is it to the nearest hospital with an accident/emergency department, and how accessible is the site for ambulances? In rural areas, it must be remembered that the nearest hospital with a casualty department may be twenty or even thirty miles from the workplace. In some kinds of work, e.g. farming, it may be extremely difficult for an ambulance to get close to the injured or sick person once it has arrived.

All the above factors should be taken into account when deciding how many first aiders should be provided. But as a rule of thumb, there should be one for every 50 employees.

'Suitable persons'

This normally means people who have attended and passed a first aid training course approved by the HSE (Health and Safety Executive) – and whose certificate is current, the normal period of validity being three years.

The employer may appoint someone else to take charge of the situation and of the first aid facilities ('appointed person') when the first aider is not there. However, this is only where the first aider is absent because of 'temporary and exceptional circumstances', which do not include holidays or cases where all the first aiders are on another shift! Enough people should be trained as first aiders to ensure cover in these circumstances.

In some cases, the risks and other factors (location, number of employees) will not be such as to justify trained first aiders. In this situation the employer may appoint (or ensure that there has been appointed) someone to take charge of the situation if someone is injured or ill, and of the first aid equipment/facilities.

To sum up, all that will be required in some cases – in addition to suitable equipment/facilities – is an appointed person. But where what is needed is a trained first aider, an appointed person can only be used as a substitute in temporary and exceptional circumstances. Although appointed persons are not first aiders as such, it is obviously a good idea if they have some relevant knowledge, especially of emergency first aid such as how to give artificial respiration, how to staunch bleeding etc.

Special short courses for appointed persons are available from the major approved training organisations such as Red Cross and St John Ambulance.

Communication

Clearly, everyone in the workplace must know what the arrangements are for first aid, otherwise precious time could be wasted in an emergency. Employers are therefore required to inform employees what the first aid arrangements are, and in particular, the location of equipment, facilities and personnel.

This is the objective – the means used is left up to the employer and will vary from organisation to organisation. Some ways of communicating these vital messages are:

- including a mention of first aid facilities in all induction training, and in any staff handbook issued to employees;
- clear notices listing first aiders/appointed persons and giving the location of the nearest first aid box or room. There may be a special internal number to call in the event of an emergency;
- prominent markings for first aid boxes/treatment rooms;
- badges for first aiders.

In keeping with the spirit of self-regulation which is fundamental to the Health and Safety at Work Act 1974, much of the decision as to what should be provided is left up to the individual employer, the objective being to ensure that whenever people are at work, help can be given should anyone fall ill or be injured.

However, to help employers interpret and comply with the Regulations, there is an important document *First Aid at Work – Approved Code of Practice and Guidance*, which is available from HMSO.

As the title suggests, this is really two documents in one – the Approved Code and the Guidance. The Approved Code has a special status in law, similar to that of the Highway Code. It is not an offence to fail to comply with it, but this could be used as evidence of failure to comply with the Regulations themselves. If an employer does not comply with the Approved Code, the onus would be on that employer to demonstrate that what had been provided was at least as good as what the Code recommends.

Equipment

All establishments should have at least one first aid box stocked to the standard laid down in Figure 4.1. The contents should be checked on a regular basis to ensure that the box is properly stocked, and nothing

Item	First aid box	Travelling kit
Guidance card	1	1
Individually wrapped sterile adhesive dressings (assorted sizes)	20	6
Sterile eye pads, with attachments	2	
Individually wrapped triangular bandages	6	
Safety pins	6	2
Medium-sized individually wrapped sterile unmedicated wound dressings (approx. 10 x 8 cm)	6	
Large sterile individually wrapped unmedicated wound dressings (approx. 13 x 9 cm)	2	
Extra large sterile individually wrapped unmedicated wound dressings (approx. 28 x 17.5 cm)	3	1

Individually wrapped moist cleaning wipes should be included in travelling first aid kits and where soap and water are not available

Figure 4.1 Contents of first aid boxes and kits

other than the recommended first aid materials should be kept in it. Small travelling first aid kits may need to be provided to people such as mobile maintenance engineers and others who are not based at a fixed site.

Depending on the numbers employed and the hazards associated with the process, it may be necessary to provide a first aid room with the following equipment and facilities:

- sink with running hot and cold water;
- drinking water 'when not available on tap' and disposable cups;
- suitable first aid equipment;
- sufficient soap;
- paper towels;
- smooth topped working surfaces;
- a suitable store for first aid materials;
- suitable refuse containers lined with a disposable plastic bag;
- a couch with a waterproof surface and frequently cleaned pillow and blankets;
- clean protective garments for use by first aiders;
- a chair;

- a bowl;
- an appropriate record book.

Records of all cases treated should be made and kept in a suitable place. An accurate record helps to protect the interests of both the individual and the employer, and is especially important if a claim for industrial injury is made – perhaps years later.

Additional considerations

We have emphasised the need for managers to carry out a thorough assessment so as to be confident that the provision made for first aid is adequate – given the actual circumstances of the workplace. Some further questions are as follows:

WHERE IS THE NEAREST HOSPITAL?

Rationalisation of the National Health Service has led to the closure of some local accident and emergency (casualty) facilities, with these services now only being available in cities and large towns. This can mean that certain workplaces – especially in rural areas – are 20 or 30 miles away from the nearest hospital with an accident/emergency department. Even in urban areas, the time it takes for an ambulance to arrive may be longer than expected, because of rush-hour traffic for example. These factors need to be taken into account in planning the workplace's first aid facilities, and a note should be kept of the nearest casualty department's location.

DO OUR ACTIVITIES CREATE ANY SPECIAL FIRST AID NEEDS?

The nature of the process may create special requirements – for example:

- provision of antidotes where there is a possibility of cyanide poisoning;
- availability of calcium gluconate gel where there is a possibility of burns from hydrogen fluoride (HF)/hydrofluoric acid;
- provision of special washing solutions for certain chemicals, e.g. isopropyl alcohol (propan-2-ol) mixed with ethylene glycol as a first aid treatment for people who have phenol or cresol splashes on their skin.

The need for these should be considered as part of any assessment carried out under the Control of Substances Hazardous to Health (COSHH) Regulations (see Chapter 2).

IS ADEQUATE DATA AVAILABLE ON THE CHEMICALS WE USE?

Suppliers' data sheets should and usually do include recommended first aid treatment for someone exposed to the chemical in question, whether by skin/eye contact, inhalation or ingestion (see Figure 4.2). It is essential that anyone giving first aid treatment has access to this information so that the right treatment can be given. A number of publications, such as Croner's *Dangerous Chemicals – First Aid Guide*, are also very useful in this respect.

Exposure effects	Contact	First aid action
Corrosive – causes burns	Skin	Drench area with water for 20 mins. Remove contaminated clothing and launder before re-use. Do not use soap. Seek medical advice.
Corrosive – may cause damage	Eyes	Irrigate thoroughly for 15–20 mins with eye wash or tap water. Gently hold eye open to ensure adequate rinsing. Take to hospital immediately.
Inhalation of spray can cause irritation	Inhalation	Remove from exposure to fresh air. Seek medical advice if irritation persists.
Corrosive – can cause internal burns	Ingestion	Remove patient's dentures, if worn. Give copious amounts of water or milk to drink. Do not give anything by mouth to an unconscious person. Seek immediate medical attention.

Figure 4.2 Typical first aid advice from manufacturer's data sheet

HAVE WE CONSIDERED THE POTENTIAL DIFFICULTIES OF GETTING FIRST AID TO PEOPLE?

The planning of first aid facilities – and the site emergency procedures – must take account of the possibility of people working in places which might prove difficult to reach quickly in an emergency. Where this is the case, there is often a double problem – getting help to the injured/sick person and extricating him/her where this turns out to be necessary. Typical situations where this might apply include:

- confined spaces, such as tanks and vessels;
- people working at heights, e.g. on roofs, or in the cabs of overhead cranes;
- maintenance work in, for example, plant rooms, lift motor rooms and roof voids.

Some frequently asked questions about first aid

ARE FIRST AIDERS ALLOWED TO GIVE OUT PAIN KILLERS SUCH AS ASPIRIN AND PARACETAMOL?

The answer to this is a definite 'no'. The dispensing of pain killers is not part of first aid, nor is it something first aiders are either trained, or should be expected, to do. Stocks of pain killers should not therefore be kept in first aid boxes. This may seem a harsh approach, bearing in mind that the drugs in question are readily available without prescription, but it is important to remember that they are nonetheless drugs that could be harmful to people suffering from certain medical conditions and that could also mask symptoms of serious illness.

One useful compromise is to use vending machines. This allows employees to obtain pain-killers for their headache, period pain etc., without placing the organisation, its managers and its first aiders in a potentially difficult situation.

WHAT IS THE PERSONAL LIABILITY OF A FIRST AIDER IF SOMETHING GOES WRONG?

A first aider has a duty of care to the person receiving first aid treatment, but the standard of care expected is that of a competent first aider, not that of a qualified nurse or doctor. A first aider trained to the standards laid down by the HSE should have no trouble in meeting this requirement.

If, however, the first aider fails to meet this duty of care (i.e. is negligent) and the person treated suffers some injury or damage to health as a result, the injured person could sue the employer rather than the first aider – in accordance with the principle of vicarious liability (see Chapter 2).

Assuming that the claim was successful, damages would be payable under the organisation's Employer's Liability Insurance policy, as for any other case of personal injury caused by one employee's negligence to a fellow employee. Legal action against the individual first aider is therefore technically possible but in practice extremely unlikely.

It is important for personnel managers to be clear about this so that first aiders who are unnecessarily concerned can be reassured – and also so that people are not put off playing an extremely valuable role as first aider because of an unjustified worry about taking on an additional personal liability.

WHAT ABOUT THE FIRST AIDER AND AIDS?

The Human Immunodeficiency Virus (HIV) – which causes AIDS – is carried in body fluids, including blood, and it is certainly possible in theory that a first aider could get AIDS through giving first aid to, and coming into contact with the body fluids of, an HIV-positive person. However, it is extremely unlikely.

In view of what is now known about AIDS, it is prudent to take certain basic precautions which will at the same time protect the first aider against the more significant danger of contracting Hepatitis from the person being treated. Contact with the casualty's body fluids should be avoided, e.g. by using disposable gloves and aprons if the patient is bleeding. Any cuts or grazes on the first aider's own skin should be covered with a dressing. Special masks are available which enable artificial respiration to be given without the first aider coming into direct contact with the casualty's mouth. Spillages of body fluids – especially blood – should be cleaned up using a dilute hypochlorite (bleach) solution.

These precautions are now commonsense, but it must be emphasised that the risk of a first aider contracting AIDS is very low. It would be quite wrong to delay or deny first aid treatment because of a fear of AIDS – this would be to magnify the risk out of all proportion. For further guidance see the CBI booklet 'AIDS and first aid'. Advice is also available from the HSE's Employment Nursing Advisory Service (contactable through HSE Area Offices).

I HAVE HEARD OF SHORT COURSES COVERING WHAT TO DO IN THE EVENT OF SOMEONE SUFFERING A HEART ATTACK AT WORK. ARE THESE OF VALUE?

This book stresses that coronary heart disease is the major cause of premature death in the UK. If someone suffers a heart attack at work, their life can be saved by someone who has been trained in cardiopulmonary resuscitation (CPR) and who can then take action to maintain a supply of oxygenated blood to the patient's brain until further help arrives.

These courses are therefore extremely valuable, although two points must be stressed. Firstly, people who have been on them are only trained in what to do in the case of a heart attack, and they should not be considered qualified first aiders. For this, attendance on a recognised course and regular follow-up training is necessary, as outlined above. Secondly, when a person has a heart attack, every second counts. Therefore this training is only going to achieve its full potential if at least one person in each department – and preferably more – can be trained. If there is any delay in getting trained help to the patient, the whole point of the exercise may be lost.

The courses are run by a number of bodies including the British Red Cross and St John Ambulance.

Doctors and nurses

So far, this chapter has concentrated on first aid, the basic treatment service which all employers must provide by law. However, many organisations provide an acute care service which goes beyond the minimum set out in the First Aid Regulations, and indeed, the treatment of injuries and illnesses arising at work is a significant function within an overall occupational health service or corporate healthcare programme.

Nurse-based treatment services are frequently provided on larger sites, and doctors may be available as well – either employed or retained by the organisation. Even where there is no formal occupational health service as such, most organisations maintain some contact with local NHS hospitals and find it useful to retain a local GP who will then see employees on a referral basis.

It is important to emphasise that, where there is an on-site treatment service, it in no way replaces the GP, who has the prime responsibility for the patients on his or her list. That said, these services do offer a convenient facility to the employee, contribute to employees' perception that their employer is humane and caring, and may improve efficiency by minimising the individual's time away from work when a consultation is needed.

However, while treatment is a significant part of what an occupational health service does, there is a danger that the approach can become a reactive one, in which too much stress is placed on dealing with problems that arise (whether of injury or illness) and not enough on a preventive, pro-active approach.

It cannot make economic sense to have a highly-trained nurse sitting in the treatment room or health centre waiting for someone to come in for treatment or advice. Nor does it make sense from the point of view of the individual's job satisfaction. The trend in the last few years has therefore been away from this approach towards one in which the emphasis is on preventing the problems occurring in the first place rather than in dealing with them once they have occurred. There are a number of related trends in workplace healthcare and these are looked at in more detail in Chapter 12 in the context of the overall management of healthcare programmes.

Private medical insurance (PMI)

It is estimated that six million people in the UK (12 per cent of the population) are now covered by some form of PMI, and of these 70 per cent receive it as part of their benefits package, with their employer either subsidising or meeting the total costs of the scheme.

The market is dominated by two provident bodies: BUPA (British United Provident Association) and PPP (Private Patients' Plan), although an increasing number of general insurers now offer PMI schemes.

Quite apart from the advantage of being able to secure rapid, private care for employees who fall ill and require hospital treatment, PMI is an attractive option to employers, because its perceived value as a benefit is high in relation to its actual cost.

In looking at the options facing the corporate buyer of PMI, the number of employees who will be covered is the key factor. As this increases, so does the number of financing options and the overall complexity of the package. It is also important to note that the greater the number of employees in the scheme, the more attractive 'self-funding' becomes, with a corresponding reduction in the insurance element of the scheme. Thus, in a large company scheme covering many thousands of employees, there may be little insurance as such, with claims being met from internal resources, possibly managed as an employees' medical trust.

The increasing complexity of private healthcare options has led to the emergence of a type of service organisation which is new to the UK but which has been common in the USA for some years – the Third Party Administrator or TPA.

The best known TPAs in the UK are Medisure (based in Bristol) and Health Care Management (based in Slough). They specialise in tailoring private healthcare packages to suit the needs of the organisation in question. They are not insurers themselves, but have expert knowledge of the insurance market and can build into the scheme whatever insurance element is appropriate.

In addition to setting up the scheme in the first place, they provide a claims management service and may also be able to offer facilities such as employee helplines. The range of options available is likely to increase still further in the future, and specialist knowledge will help identify the scheme which best meets the organisation's needs – and gives the best value for money.

Disaster planning

One of the hardest of all management disciplines, disaster planning requires imagination and insight to foresee the 'catastrophe' which may be very improbable, but if it were to happen, could have very serious consequences not only for individuals but for the whole organisation.

Many organisations confine their emergency planning to fire procedures and safety matters such as what to do in the event of a chemical spill, but careful thought will show that there are also some potential health-related 'disasters', such as:

- sudden serious illness of an employee or visitor;
- outbreak of food poisoning;
- outbreak of Legionnaire's disease.

Clearly, the first thought is for prevention – minimising the risk of these things happening in the first place. Incidentally, one of the benefits of committing proper resources to emergency planning is to make the emergencies themselves less likely – because of the improved awareness and foresight that the process of emergency planning generates. However, where the preventive approach has not been successful, it is far easier to cope if proper procedures have been thought out (and if possible, practised) beforehand. The action required will consist not only of that necessary to help the victim, but also things such as informing relatives and dealing with the press.

A detailed treatment of emergency planning for organisations is beyond the scope of this book, but it may be helpful to stress the following general points which are applicable to all emergency planning – whether for health issues or others:

- procedures need to be comprehensive;
- key people need to be identified, along with their responsibilities. When an emergency happens, it will waste precious time if who is to do what then has to be decided;
- adequate medical advice (e.g. retained medical adviser/occupational physician) needs to be available;
- the procedures need to be as simple as possible, and should preferably be documented in some ready reference form (time being of the essence once a problem occurs);
- the contents of the emergency plan must be communicated

effectively to those who would be involved in implementing it. Practices should be held to reinforce the training and identify areas for possible improvement;

- the emergency plan must be kept up-to-date.

The importance of the last point is illustrated by what happened in one company, where emergency action was co-ordinated through the security department, which was the first point of contact in the event of any emergency on site.

A decision was made to transfer the responsibility for site security matters to a specialist contractor, but in doing this, the role of security staff within the emergency plan was forgotten. When an accident occurred on site in which an employee was overcome by fumes and had to be taken to hospital, misunderstanding occurred because line managers assumed that security would take certain action which in fact the security men on duty did not know it was their responsibility to take. This emphasises the need for regular reviews of emergency arrangements so that any changes – made necessary by re-organisation, for example – can be built in.

CHECKLIST

- Do we provide adequate first aid, and in particular, suitable facilities and properly trained first aiders?
- Is there adequate cover at all times, including shift work, holiday periods, weekend working etc?
- Have we considered the need for portable first aid kits in our vehicles?
- Does everyone know what the first aid arrangements are?
- Have the advantages of training people in Cardiopulmonary Resuscitation been investigated?
- Is there an effective system to ensure that first aid boxes, emergency eye washes etc. are regularly inspected, replenished as necessary and available for immediate use?
- Do we know where the nearest accident and emergency hospital is?
- Are there any processes which create special first aid requirements?
- Has the full range of private medical insurance options been considered?
- Do we have an emergency plan for all our sites? Does it include health emergencies, and would key people such as supervisors, receptionists and site security staff know what to do in an emergency?

CHAPTER 5
Using Professional Services

As the horizons of corporate healthcare have broadened, so the need for specialist professional skills has developed. It is no longer possible for a single individual to provide the full range of expertise necessary to take care of all aspects of employee health. Since it is unlikely that all necessary skills will exist within the organisation, employers need to have up-to-date knowledge of relevant external professional services.

Appropriate services include general as well as occupational health, and are likely to include some skills from the safety profession. Once essential legal requirements have been met, the priorities will relate to the main health risks to which employees are exposed. Additional reporting and analysis of accidents and ill health may be needed to establish exactly where the priorities lie.

Identification of the most appropriate professional skills requires up-to-date knowledge of a wide range of specialist activities. These include occupational hygienists, ergonomists, occupational psychologists, and physiotherapists. Maintaining knowledge of their services, and co-ordinating internal and external health services can be time-consuming and should be a clearly identified responsibility in its own right.

In the first chapter it was noted that the business of providing healthcare services to employees is a *multidisciplinary* activity. There is simply no individual skill that addresses all of the factors which influence health at work. It is therefore most unlikely that all but the very largest organisations can provide in-house the whole range of expertise necessary to tackle a full corporate healthcare programme. This chapter considers some of the many professional skills which might be needed, and comments on the ways in which those services can be obtained and used to best effect. As Figure 5.1 indicates, these skills can be directed

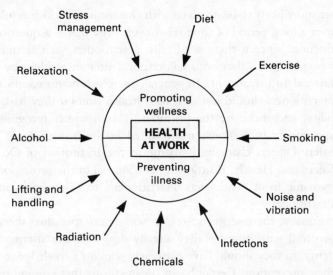

Figure 5.1 Examples of the range of issues that can be tackled in a company health programme

at the prevention of work-induced illness, or at the promotion of issues designed to maintain good health.

What are the limits of corporate healthcare?

There is growing recognition that the improving standards of health which have marked the last century, result not just from developments in medicine, but from advances in food hygiene, housing standards, sewerage engineering, etc. The same is true of developments in corporate healthcare, where engineering systems, training programmes, and industrial design have all played their part in raising health standards at work.

So what should be included in a corporate healthcare programme? The answer is *anything* that genuinely contributes to employee health. There would really be no point in embarking on an expensive screening programme because it was 'proper' healthcare, if a cheaper company health campaign would achieve greater results. The challenge then, is more to decide on priorities, than on what does or doesn't constitute healthcare. However, one boundary line which does sometimes cause problems is that between health at work, and safety.

As has already been discussed, safety is generally concerned with acute issues which might result in injury. Health practitioners at work are more likely to be involved with chronic issues which result in illness over a long period of time. However, even that is a questionable distinction, since if there are health practitioners such as nurses at the workplace, it is they who will respond after an accident by providing first aid and treatment. In general, there can be no reason why *safety* practitioners should not deal with health issues if they have the capability, and those are the priorities. This is widely recognised by the appropriate professions, and resulted in the Institution of Industrial Safety Officers changing its name to the Institution of Occupational Safety and Health. A little later the journal of the profession changed its name from 'The Safety Practitioner', to 'The Safety and Health Practitioner'.

Equally, there seems no reason why *health* specialists should not be involved with safety – they already deal with the aftermath of accidents, so they should have extremely relevant knowledge to advise on their prevention. Certainly, in organisations that employ both safety and health professionals, it would seem essential to ensure they are both within the same reporting structure – so that their activities are co-ordinated and that both work towards the same objectives.

However, the loose labels 'health' and 'safety', cover a multitude of special skills. Figure 5.2 shows some of the professional bodies whose activities contribute to the health of people at work – some addresses can be found in Appendix 1. This illustrates the enormous diversity of the subject, and the importance of ensuring that the key role in corporate healthcare is one of co-ordination. In other words, someone

---

Organisations involved with preventive healthcare

Action on Smoking and Health	Family Heart Association
Alcohol Concern	Health Education Authority
Alcoholics Anonymous	Health Promotion Research Trust
British Heart Foundation	Health and Safety Executive
British Medical Association	Institute of Alcohol Studies
British Occupational Hygiene Society	Institution of Occupational Safety and Health
British Lung Foundation	Institute of Occupational Health
British Diabetic Association	Institute of Occupational Hygienists
Cancer Research Campaign	Royal Society of Medicine
Centre for Health Economics	Royal College of Physicians
Chest, Heart and Stroke Association	Society of Occupational Medicine
Coronary Prevention Group	Sports Council

Figure 5.2

---

with overall responsibility for the healthcare programme needs to be reasonably detached from its day to day practice, and to ensure that the right skills are brought to bear on the current priorities.

For the purposes of reviewing the range of professional services available, it is necessary to introduce some classification, and therefore three general categories will be considered:

1. General healthcare, covering aspects of health which are not necessarily directly related to the working environment, but which are nevertheless genuine health issues for people at work.
2. Occupational healthcare, dealing with those health issues which actually result from the conditions of work, or would not arise in the absence of the work.
3. Safety, covering acute incidents, whether caused by the working environment or not, which threaten the life and health of employees.

General healthcare

Much of the subject matter of this book is concerned with introducing aspects of general health into the workplace. The justification is straightforward – these are the things that most affect working people, and will therefore give the greatest 'return' if tackled by employers. These are also the issues which raise most debate in the field of corporate healthcare, and when they are opposed, it is normally on one of two grounds: Firstly that issues of general health have nothing to do with the employer, and indeed that employers who introduce such issues could be interfering with things that are none of their business; and secondly that general health issues are dealt with by State services, usually the National Health Service, and that activities by employers could be a wasteful duplication of State services, and possibly be in conflict with them.

These are issues that employers and employees will need to discuss openly and resolve together. However, there are also some persuasive arguments *for* including a broad range of healthcare issues in company programmes:

1. While it is true that non-occupational health issues are the province of the NHS, there is limited scope for preventive healthcare within the present system. This is largely a question of resources, with the current emphasis being on treatment services.
2. The employer is in a unique position to inform, advise and persuade on issues of health; employers are the leading educators of adults.

They have a captive audience and consume the major part of most people's waking time. If employers do not introduce preventive healthcare programmes then, for the majority of people, no-one will.

3. The health issues which most affect employers by resulting in absenteeism, work inefficiency, and the premature illness and death of employees, are usually general, rather than specific to occupations.
4. In practice general health issues are inseparable from the everyday activities of nearly all employers. Company procedures will generally require attention to hygiene, restrictions on smoking, reporting of illness etc. Relatively limited extensions of such approaches will greatly enhance the benefits.

So what aspects of general healthcare can the employer contribute to? And how is it done? The chapters of this book indicate some of today's priorities. Coronary heart disease is the UK's leading cause of death and is associated with risk factors, many of which are controllable. Many cancer deaths could be prevented if there was more widespread knowledge about their causes. The severity of much respiratory illness could be reduced given better understanding of its nature and causes. Strokes could be reduced if preventive healthcare measures were followed. AIDS can be prevented if there is knowledge of its transmission and an understanding of precautionary measures. These and other causes of illness and death can be dealt with in a healthcare programme which includes information and early detection of disease.

Doctors and nurses

Perhaps the most usual way of bringing such issues into the workplace is by means of the 'Company Doctor'. This is often a part-time role, possibly taken by a local General Practitioner. The doctor can organise health publicity programmes, give talks on health matters of interest, and also be available for one-to-one consultation. The doctor can also provide a direct service to management by advising on health aspects of company policy, and indicating significant health issues for the workforce as a whole. It is important to emphasise that the direct contact between the doctor and an employee will be strictly confidential unless clearly agreed otherwise.

The company doctor can also provide valuable health screening services, which are discussed in detail in Chapter 3. Preventive health screens have become increasingly attractive as an in-company service with the arrival of a range of new technology. Particularly important are the desk-top blood analysers, and computer software programs for health screening. The desk top analysers enable company doctors and nurses to check blood glucose, blood cholesterol levels, etc. in just a few minutes. The new software programs have health screening protocols built in, and enable health screening reports to be printed, lifestyle programmes to be prepared, and all data to be statistically analysed. Such screening exercises are likely to be more productive than pre-employment screening, in the past often the only screening undertaken in-house. Pre-employment screening may be important where certain medical conditions must be met if the individual is to do the job safely. But in general, physical 'hands-on' screening of prospective employees results in too low a rejection rate to be cost effective. In other words the cost saved by not taking an unsuitable employee, is less than the cost incurred in running the screening programme.

An alternative 'general' healthcare employee with the ability to undertake a wide range of duties, is a nurse. The image of the company nurse has suffered from the common view that she or he is someone who sits in a surgery waiting for opportunities to dispense bandages or aspirins. This indeed may still be the case in some situations, but is now a rarity. Company nurses are extremely effective at getting into the workplace and promoting preventive healthcare. Nurses often organise exercise classes, weight watching programmes, no-smoking publicity, etc. They also increasingly deal with safety matters – on the grounds that they are better employed preventing accidents than treating them. The majority of health screening programmes can also be run by nurses, who often have outstanding communication and counselling skills and are therefore particularly effective at using screening results to encourage desirable changes in lifestyle.

Specialists

There is a wide variety of other healthcare practitioners who are increasingly providing some or all of their service within organisations. Examples are given in the following paragraphs.

Nutrition

Nutritionists specialise in giving advice on food and diet. This is important in preventive healthcare for a number of reasons. Firstly, diet is closely linked with health. A great deal of work has been done on this subject in recent years by organisations such as NACNE – the National Advisory Committee on Nutrition Education. As a result of knowledge about the link between various food components and disease (for example saturated fat and heart disease, sugar and tooth decay, salt and hypertension), some clear recommendations have been made about desirable changes to the average British diet. In summary, these are:

- a reduction in the total energy derived from dietary fat;
- a reduction in the intake of saturated fat;
- an increase in the intake of complex carbohydrate, starchy foods, and fibre;
- a decrease in sugar intake;
- a decrease in salt intake.

Other reasons for the importance of nutritional advice relate to the ability of diet to influence other factors, which themselves affect health or well-being. The most obvious example is weight – an important feature of self-image, as well as being itself a coronary risk factor, and a factor in the development of personal fitness. For all these reasons, diet is a vital part of most preventive healthcare programmes. It is a complicated subject with new information appearing all the time, and certainly justifies specialist help. Nutritionists working in companies can advise employees and managers, support other specialists such as doctors, and assist with issues such as menus for the staff canteen.

Dentistry

Dentists provide a service which needs little explanation – though it is perhaps worth pointing out how significant a move the dental profession has made from reactive to preventive treatment. Much of the work of dentists is now based on preventing tooth decay rather than treating it, and in a short space of time this approach has achieved impressive results – with tooth decay falling by about 30 per cent amongst young children over a ten year period (although factors such as water fluoridation and reduced sugar consumption are also relevant here). However, preventive dentistry came too late for many of Britain's adults, a quarter of whom have no natural teeth. Of the remainder, the vast majority have some level of tooth decay, resulting in the national expenditure of £800 million per year on treatment. The benefits of providing this service in-house are clear. Much time is taken off work to visit the dentist – and most of this is travelling time to and from the dentist rather than treatment time. So a facility at work is both a valuable benefit, as well as a saving in productive time for the employer. To be realistic, this is probably only a consideration for those employers who have large numbers of employees on a single site since an investment is needed in space and facilities, as well as dentist time. However, when circumstances do permit, occupational dentistry is undoubtedly a healthcare service of benefit to the vast majority of the workforce.

Physiotherapy

Physiotherapists are frequently involved in corporate healthcare programmes, introducing exercise, heat and massage to the treatment of pain and sprains. Again this is directly relevant to large numbers of working people. According to a Consumers' Association survey, back pain affects about half the adult population at some time, with one in three adults being affected in any twelve month period. It features strongly in all analysis of company sickness absence, alongside colds and flu, as a major cause of lost time. An Office of Health Economics study suggested that back problems cost British Industry some one billion pounds per year through lost production. Of course, not all of this could be eliminated by physiotherapy. But there is scope for a real contribution, as well as providing treatment following accidents and injuries.

Optometry

Opticians offer a popular service when provided in companies. They enable eye tests to be obtained conveniently and, if the employer is paying, without incurring the charge now levied through high-street opticians. As well as identifying visual defects, the optician will screen for glaucoma – a disease resulting in pressure within the eye which destroys the visual nerve fibres. Glaucoma occurs mainly after the age of 50 and is responsible for over a quarter of all blindness after the age of 45. Eye testing is appropriate for all employees who need good eyesight to work properly, for example because they drive, operate precision machinery, or use visual display units. Eye screening is then important, not because eyesight will be damaged by the work, but because working with defective eyesight might result in headaches and, in some cases, risks to the employee and others.

Chiropody

Chiropodists often provide services through employers. Modern chiropodists are specialists capable of providing a comprehensive foot health service. This includes treatment of foot deformities, long term foot care, and treatment to give short term relief of painful symptoms. Chiropody includes the use of various therapeutic techniques, including minor surgery, and the fitting of corrective footwear appliances. Chiropodists are also trained to recognise medical conditions which show themselves in the feet. These include circulation disorders, diabetes, and diseases causing ulceration.

Psychology

Psychologists are increasingly working with businesses, often dealing with a wide range of problems including stress – covered in detail in Chapter 6 – as well as job design, and selection of the right person for a position. Stress is now recognised to be one of *the* key health issues for employers. Stress is often caused by pressures of work, and takes its toll through reduced working efficiency, and by contributing to the development of a wide range of illnesses. These include stomach disorders, skin problems, and heart disease. Trained stress counsellors and psychologists aim to identify the causes of stress, and introduce stress reduction programmes which are suited to the individual. These might include training in relaxation techniques, use of exercise and meditation, as well as dealing directly with the cause of the stress, perhaps by taking a more philosophical approach to it.

There has been considerable growth in the provision of stress reduction programmes for employees in the USA, and the comprehensive service dealing with this has become known as the Employee Assistance Programme, or EAP. EAPs usually provide some sort of 'hot line' contact for employees experiencing stress. This would probably be telephone access to a counsellor or psychologist, who would assist wherever possible, and might then arrange further face to face counselling sessions. The EAP programme could also include general training and advice for employees in stress management, and training for managers in the recognition of early warning signs of stress in their employees. EAPs are now being introduced into Great Britain, though as yet there is uncertainty about how effective they will be, and how many employees will be willing to deal with their problems in this way.

Occupational healthcare

It has already been observed that one of the major developments in corporate healthcare programmes is the growing willingness of employers to become involved in aspects of employee health which are not directly related to work. However, some health problems *are* the result of work, and these too must be dealt with in the corporate health plan. Indeed, as suggested as one of the principles of health screening in Chapter 3, dealing with work-induced health problems is likely to be a priority. There are three main reasons for this:

1. Health problems which result from the conditions of the working environment have the potential for solution by environmental, rather than biological, measures. Thus a problem of dermatitis, say, might be resolved by substitution of the sensitising or irritant chemical, rather than treatment of the affected individuals. This is obviously more satisfactory, since it is a guaranteed permanent solution and even the early stages of illness are avoided.
2. If an employer knows, or should know, that working conditions are creating risks to health, then there is a legal duty to eliminate those risks – so far as is reasonably practicable.
3. Broadly-based healthcare programmes will have little credibility if the workplace itself is seen to be a health hazard.

So what sort of health problems might result from work, and require specialist attention? Typical examples are:

- chemical hazards, occurring in virtually every workplace, and now controlled by the COSHH Regulations;
- noise, affecting millions of employees through noise-induced deafness, and controlled by the Noise at Work Regulations;
- vibration, causing circulation disorders such as 'white-finger', resulting from prolonged contact with vibrating objects such as hand tools;
- radiation, causing burns, sickness and cancer if exposure is prolonged and excessive;
- sick building syndrome, resulting in a variety of symptoms such as nausea, rashes and headaches, and probably arising from a range of conditions commonly found in modern buildings;
- infections, such as Legionnaire's disease, resulting from poorly maintained cooling towers and other water systems;
- repetitive strain injury, causing pain and immobility, and resulting from work that requires fast, repetitive movements;
- sprains and strains, caused by working in awkward and uncomfortable conditions.

The above list illustrates the range of health issues that might directly result from the working environment. None of them is a new health problem, though the importance of many of them was underestimated for many years because of the difficulty of linking cause with effect. Where they exist they are a priority for attention, but are likely to require specialist input from someone who knows the exact legal requirements, and who can measure the magnitude of the problem and introduce the necessary control measures – a specialist in occupational health.

Occupational doctors and nurses

A specific branch of the medical profession is dedicated to dealing with health problems resulting from work. Doctors and nurses working in this field will have obtained basic general qualifications, and then gone through a further period of training to qualify as occupational specialists. This would typically be demonstrated by doctors becoming Associates or Members of the Faculty of Occupational Medicine, and by nurses obtaining a Diploma or Certificate in Occupational Nursing through a course of training following their Registered General Nurse qualification.

Occupational doctors and nurses possess a wide range of skills which enable them to identify and respond to the diseases of occupations. They are sensitive to the symptoms which might be caused by, say, exposure to chemicals, and are familiar with the appropriate treatments. They can assess the working environment for health risks, and assist in risk reduction measures. Just as importantly, they understand the way in which employers work – they should know how to relate to employees and employee representatives such as trade unions. They will be able to contribute at health and safety committee meetings. They will deal with relevant external bodies such as the Health and Safety Executive. They will prepare appropriate company policies and procedures.

None of the above should be taken to read that, in the field of workplace health, occupational doctors and nurses will do *everything*. This subject is now multi-disciplinary, and there is no-one who can do everything. So a vital additional quality for these specialists is the possession of good inter-personal skills. These will be needed for work with plant engineers, trainers, personnel specialists, and others whose work is essential to the maintenance of employee health.

Occupational hygienists

In Chapter 1 it was noted that much of the progress made in dealing with workplace health issues was due to the work of occupational hygienists. Occupational hygiene is specifically concerned with the measurement and control of occupational health hazards. It is a highly technical discipline, as well as being extremely practical, and good hygienists are in great demand. A number of particular approaches are adopted by occupational hygienists, which are often reflected in modern health and safety legislation. The COSHH Regulations in particular are often said to embody the essential principles of occupational hygiene, which include the following points.

Measurement of environmental contaminants such as noise, dust, fumes, radiation, vibration, etc. is usually far from straightforward and involves complex sampling and analysis equipment. Some of this is designed to be actually worn by operators, and some must be capable of use in hazardous environments. Environmental measurement is complicated by the many variables which are associated with any contaminant. Noise, for example, varies from second to second in the average workplace. The intensity of noise varies, as does the frequency of its wavelength. Noise also varies with position – very relevant to anyone who moves from place to place at work. Dust contamination has similarly complex variables. As well as varying in concentration from time to time and place to place, the composition of dust varies, as does the shape and size of individual dust particles. All of these factors are relevant to an assessment of how great a risk to health will be presented by a given working environment, and it is in making this assessment that the occupational hygienist specialises.

Substitution (replacing hazardous conditions with safer ones), is likely to be the first objective of the occupational hygienist. This will reduce the health risk permanently and eliminate the need for elaborate control or protection measures. Occupational hygienists are familiar with those substitutions which will reduce risks to health – for example noisy machines with quieter ones, or harmful solvents with safer ones. These substitutions are not always expensive, and may actually save money since contamination is often caused by wasted energy or chemicals which are saved with safer equipment. A recent hygiene survey in a large plant found a number of circumstances where hazardous, and expensive, organic solvents could actually be replaced by water – no-one had ever before queried whether the solvents were really necessary.

Control of environmental hazards is a major part of any occupational hygienist's role. Again, this is likely to be highly technical with a range of options, all of which need to be evaluated for their effectiveness and their cost implications. A favoured approach where it is feasible is often enclosure, in which the health hazard is literally boxed-in. However, the design of enclosures is never simple, since there will be special structural requirements, and the enclosure will have to allow for access and maintenance, and for the input and output of raw materials, energy, and product. Other control options will include ventilation and point extraction systems – requiring extremely careful design and installation if they are to achieve the desired effect.

Protection of employees with suitable protective clothing is often said to be the hygienist's last resort – only to be used when substitution and control have failed. This may be the case, but it is nevertheless often necessary. Occupational hygienists will be familiar with the range of options for protection, and will again wish to consider issues of effectiveness and cost. This too, is a very technical field. Respiratory protectors come in all shapes and sizes, from face masks to total body suits, some with air supply, others fitted with dust or fume filters. The selection, fitting, testing and training associated with protective clothing is a specialist field which must be dealt with correctly if they are to effectively remove hazards to health at work.

Ergonomists

Ergonomics is a relatively new science, developed mainly after the Second World War. Its name is made up from the Greek words for work and management, and it is the study of the physical and psychological factors that affect the efficiency of machines and systems used by humans. Ergonomics has many applications in issues affecting health at work, and is increasingly used as attention is directed to factors such as posture and illumination. A good example is the challenge of introducing widespread use of visual display units (VDUs) without risk to health. After much study, including investigation of possible risks to pregnancy, it has become clear that the major problems of extended VDU use are likely to relate to ergonomic factors. The main needs are to ensure proper positioning, seating, layout etc., coupled with patterns of work which allow efficient work without undue strain. Such issues are the province of the ergonomist, who can advise on the whole range of conditions which affect working efficiency. There is little doubt that the most effective involvement of ergonomists in corporate healthcare programmes is at the earliest possible stage – when changes to design, layout, decor, etc. can be made without major upheaval. In such circumstances the ergonomist has a major role to play in enhancing health at work.

Safety

It was observed earlier that the line dividing health from safety is not

a clear one, and that if the objective of a corporate healthcare programme is to keep people alive and healthy, it will have to incorporate
some safety issues. In any case, the development of health plans at
work will benefit by borrowing some approaches long established by
safety practitioners. It is interesting to see how often this is not done,
even in companies with safety *and* health resources. A good example
is the keeping and analysing of records. Most organisations keep
detailed records of accidents, and present detailed statistics of the
causes of the accidents, their nature, the resulting time off, trends,
severity, and so on. However, it is quite rare for the same degree of
analysis to be applied to illness. Most companies, for example, would
be unable to say how much sickness absence resulted from back pain,
or colds, or heart disease – even though these are certain to be more
significant issues than absence from injuries.

So if safety specialists are to be involved in the corporate healthcare
programme, who are they? And what will be their priorities? Safety
professionals come from many walks of life. Unlike medical practitioners, they are unlikely to have started by qualifying in their field
and could well have gained experience and qualifications in some other
area – such as engineering – before being drawn to safety. There are
then a number of training options they might pursue, including
degree-level courses at Aston university. For most general safety practitioners, the mark of professional competence and experience is
Membership of the Institution of Safety and Health. The Institution
also keeps a register of active and competent members – designated as
Registered Safety Practitioners.

To decide on the priorities for safety issues it is worth looking at
approximate figures for the severity of accidents in Great Britain,
measured by annual death rates, for the three main accident locations:

accidents at work	400 deaths per year
accidents at home	5000 deaths per year
road accidents	6000 deaths per year

The figures for injuries are, of course, much larger, but show the same
sort of percentage distribution between the three categories. The main
observation to be made here is that, just as with health, the greatest
benefit in tackling safety issues at work may come from reducing risks
outside the workplace. Again this raises familiar questions – 'is it the
employer's business?', etc., and again there may be legal reasons for
dealing with work risks first. But there is no doubt that, if the aim is
to reduce employee accidents, then at least some of the training, etc.

should be directed at the environment away from work – since that is where employees are most at risk.

Home accidents

Home accidents, of course, affect more than the working population, and children and the elderly play a large part in the statistics. However, even these figures can benefit from programmes run at work, since employees who are trained in home safety will be likely to reduce home risks both for themselves and others. It is probable that the main contribution to home safety within a corporate programme will be training and education. Many people are simply not aware of the main domestic risks, and are extremely interested and receptive towards information and advice on the subject. The information might range from basic first aid and emergency instruction (how to deal with kitchen fires, how to treat burns, falls, etc.), to advice on actually reducing accident risks at home. A breakdown of the major causes of accidental death at home will indicate likely priorities:

falls	3000 deaths per year
fires	600 deaths per year
poisoning	500 deaths per year
suffocation	300 deaths per year

Other, though lesser causes of death and injury include electrocution and cuts from broken window glass.

Road accidents

Road accidents present much the greatest risk of accidental injury or death for working people. Despite this fact most people, even if their work involves driving, receive no training in safe driving techniques or, indeed, any driving training at all once they have passed their driving test. It is worth noting that the one driving group which *does* have additional training – the drivers of heavy goods vehicles – produce the lowest rate of accidents of any vehicle category in Great Britain.

As in dealing with home safety, the best approach for employers is probably that of providing information, support and training. Training in safer driving (sometimes known as 'defensive driving') is widely available, and increasingly provided by employers. Such training strongly emphasises the importance of safe driving, demonstrates where the risks are greatest, and uses a variety of techniques to improve safe driving skills. Ideally, the training should include some on the road experience with the instructor, though much of the training can be classroom based. The aim is to make permanent changes to long-established patterns of behaviour, including:

- increasing the distance between you and the vehicle in front;
- reducing speed;
- avoiding all alcohol when driving;
- controlling skids;
- being aware of other traffic.

Such training has the surprising potential for reducing accident rates by more than at first seems theoretically possible. The reason is that defensively trained drivers can avoid accidents which would not in any case have been their fault – by responding 'defensively' to other dangerous road users. Training drivers to drive can meet with resistance since virtually all drivers already believe their driving skills are better than average. However, once this barrier is overcome, the training is invariably enjoyed and appreciated, with great benefit to the employees, to other road users, and to the employer.

This checklist is designed to indicate the potential for using additional professional skills in the development and maintenance of corporate healthcare programmes.

- Does our reporting structure ensure that all professional skills relating to employee health are properly co-ordinated?
- Do we utilise professional skills which assist employees in protecting their health outside as well as inside the workplace?
- Are appropriate skills co-opted as they are needed, to assist with special projects, health campaigns, etc.?
- Does someone have the responsibility for keeping in touch with developments in health at work, new research findings, etc., and seeking specialist advice on them when necessary?
- Have we given consideration to bringing health specialists into the workplace to save the time of employees away from work, and as an employment benefit?
- Do we fully document and analyse all causes of absence and ill health, as a basis for determining the need for particular specialist input?
- Are specialists in the organisation fully encouraged to progress their professional training, to keep up to date with developments, and to develop additional specialist skills if they are relevant to work?
- Do we encourage external professional consultants such as occupational hygienists, ergonomists, driving trainers, etc., to present ideas about ways in which they could help the organisation?
- Do we ensure that the professionals we use in this area have all the qualifications and experience they require?
- Do we go out of our way to support specialists who wish to join and participate in the work of professional bodies involved with corporate health (for example, by paying professional subscriptions, hosting branch meetings, etc.?)

LOOKING AFTER CORPORATE HEALTH

CHAPTER 6
Stress

Stress continues to receive much publicity, not only as a risk factor for coronary heart disease, but also as a major cause of absence from work. It is not simply pressure on the individual; up to a certain point, stress is a positive and necessary thing. Mental and physical problems arise when the pressure exceeds the individual's ability to cope – and this in turn is affected by personality and other factors. Managers need to be aware of stress in themselves and in others, and a number of techniques are available for managing stress at both individual and corporate levels.

Of all the health issues covered in this book, stress is one of the most difficult for managers to analyse. We all know what stress feels like, but it is very hard to define and even more difficult to quantify. This is true at the personal level (how much stress am I under?) and at the organisational level (how much of our absenteeism is due to stress and what is it costing?). Something that is hard to define and even harder to measure is likely to prove exceedingly difficult to manage. A further complication is the wide diversity in the causes and effects of stress.

Causes in the workplace may include:

- relatively straightforward physical factors, such as noise, poor lighting or inadequate ventilation;
- workload and pressure problems like those facing the manager who has two equally important pieces of work to finish against what seem impossible deadlines, or who is stuck in a traffic jam as the time set for an important meeting with a valuable client draws closer and closer;
- work which is insufficiently challenging, allowing the individual little scope for a feeling of personal pride;
- a company culture in which climbing to the top is

inseparable from treading down your colleagues, and in which aggression is more highly prized than empathy.

Effects may be mental or physical, or a combination of these. In this chapter, we explore what stress is and how it is caused, and make some practical suggestions for dealing with it, both at a personal and a corporate level.

What is stress?

One of the problems in defining stress is that there are many things both outside and within us which impose pressures, and all these may be forms of stress. Here it must be emphasised that, in this sense, stress is not a bad thing. Indeed, it has been said that life without stress would be no life at all, and if it were possible to eliminate all stress, we might just as well be dead.

So to be more precise, what we are concerned about is not so much a question of whether, but of how much. What we are worried about is the point at which the stress exceeds the ability of the individual to cope with it.

This point is crucial to understanding stress, but of course it is not an easy point to define. At any one time, we are subject to stresses from a number of sources, including work, and these vary continuously. At the same time, people react to different pressures in different ways, according to their personality, skills and experience. Mrs A may feel no qualms at all about taking a damaged piece of goods back to the shop and asking for a refund, while Mr B goes into agonies of worry about how the request will be received and wonders if it would not simply be better to do nothing. Yet Mr B is a keen member of his amateur dramatic society, and feels not worry but an exhilarating buzz of excitement as he steps onto the stage on the first night of the latest production, a situation in which Mrs A may well feel like a lamb being taken to slaughter.

The physical effects of stress

Medical studies of stress have tended to emphasise the physiological effects of stress, for the changes which occur to the body in a stressful situation are readily detectable and well-documented.

These changes include the release of adrenalin (and other so-called 'stress hormones') into the bloodstream, followed in turn by a number of other changes. These have been described in terms of the primitive 'fight or flight' response in which the person faced with danger gears up either to do battle with the aggressor or to make a rapid escape. When we are stressed:

- the heart beats faster, with the normal adult pulse of just over 70 beats a minute rising possibly as high as 200 beats a minute in extremely stressful conditions, and blood pressure rises;
- 'fuels' such as sugar and fats are released into the bloodstream;
- we breathe more rapidly, so that more oxygen can be carried around the body by the blood;
- changes occur in the blood itself so that it clots more readily (a protective measure in preparation for physical injury);
- the mouth dries up, and digestion is suspended as blood is diverted to the brain and the muscles;
- we sweat in anticipation of strenuous physical activity which will require a cooling mechanism to control body temperature.

Of course, these responses are perfect for the primitive man confronted with a dangerous animal, but do no good at all to the manager who is waiting to go into a difficult meeting or the sales representative who is stuck in a traffic jam. Medical studies emphasise that it is not only the inappropriateness but also the duration of these physiological responses that causes problems. If the 'alarm' state of instant readiness is prolonged – because the stress does not go away and the individual still feels threatened – then damage to health can result.

Phases of arousal

Three distinct phases of arousal can be identified. In Phase I, the body readies itself for 'fight or flight' as described above and is brought to an acute state of alertness and readiness. In Phase II, the level of arousal diminishes, but the body is still held in a tense, alert state – ready for action. In Phase III, the state of arousal and readiness has been maintained for too long and the result is exhaustion and potential damage to health. There may at this stage be indicators such as the following:

- bad temper and irritability;
- the person is unusually argumentative and may have trouble sleeping properly;
- eating habits may change;
- the person may overreact, e.g. to minor problems that he would normally take in his stride.

These indicators are important, because they may be recognised as signs of stress by others, and the individual counselled or otherwise helped as a result. One of the problems facing people who are at this stage of stress is that they may well lose the ability to see themselves objectively, and hence recognise the dangers of the situation. Nor may they be able to take action to help themselves – hence the futility of saying 'pull yourself together, everything will be alright!' to such a person.

In addition to the concept of Phases I, II and III, it may be helpful to see stress in terms of the human performance curve (see Figure 6.1).

This emphasises that the problem is not pressure itself. Up to a certain point, performance actually increases as we feel under more pressure, and in this sense stress is stimulating.

Many people find that they need the stimulus of having to get something done in a short time to work at their best. Indeed, if they did everything in a leisurely and relaxed way, they would not get as much (if anything) done!

The problems arise where the peak of the curve is reached, and thereafter, even though pressure increases, performance falls off and health may well deteriorate. It is therefore important to distinguish between 'positive stress' – which is stimulating and invigorating – and 'negative stress' – which may ultimately be destructive of both health and happiness.

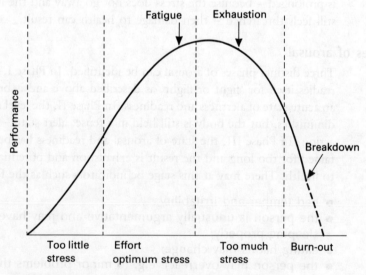

Figure 6.1 The human performance curve

In *The Complete Guide to Stress Management*, Dr Chandra Patel gives the following examples to illustrate this point:

EXAMPLES OF POSITIVE STRESS

- feeling confident we will overcome a challenge;
- feeling exhilarated and invigorated by a competitive sport;
- getting a promotion we have been waiting for;
- winning the football pools;
- being involved in a new love affair.

EXAMPLES OF NEGATIVE STRESS

- having to learn a difficult task;
- being stuck in a traffic jam;
- secretary being off sick;
- child having measles;
- computer breaking down.

Stress and illness

As stress was more closely researched, further information emerged about the links between stress and illness. In particular, it became clear that people exposed to stress, and especially those subjected to stressful life changes such as the death of a close member of the family, were far more susceptible to illness than those not so exposed.

There followed attempts to quantify the stress factors in people's lives. Of these, the best known is the Holmes and Rahe scale, in which a number of potentially stressful events – ranging from minor violation of the law up to death of spouse – are given a points score (see Figure 6.2). People are asked to identify which events have happened in their lives within the last 12 months and to total the corresponding scores. The higher the total, the greater the level of stress and the greater the susceptibility to illness.

It will be seen that the scoring system aims to measure the amount of adjustment the individual is having to make, depending on the frequency and severity of the changes in the person's life. This ties in with Holmes and Rahe's findings that the greater the amount of social readjustment required, the greater the likelihood of illness. It also helps us to recognise that much stress is not work-related.

Work done since has emphasised the importance of looking beyond the actual nature and number of events and understanding how the individual sees the event. It is a common experience that people react in ways that do not necessarily relate to the severity of the event – the

Event	Stress points
Death of spouse	100
Divorce	73
Marital separation	65
Jail term	63
Death of a close family member	63
Personal injury or illness	53
Marriage	50
Fired at work	47
Marital reconciliation	45
Retirement	45
Change in family member's health	44
Pregnancy	40
Sex difficulties	39
Addition to family	39
Business readjustment	39
Change in financial state	38
Death of a close friend	37
Change to a different line of work	36
Change in number of arguments	35
Taking out a large mortgage or loan	31
Foreclosure on mortgage or loan	30
Change in work responsibilities	29
Son or daughter leaving home	29
Trouble with in-laws	29
Outstanding personal achievement	28
Spouse begins or stops work	26
Starting or finishing school	26
Change in living conditions	25
Revision of personal habits	24
Trouble with boss	23
Change in work hours or conditions	20
Change in residence	20
Change in school	20
Change in recreational habits	19
Change in church activities	19
Change in social activities	18
Taking out a small mortgage or loan	17
Change in sleeping habits	16
Change in number of family gatherings	15
Change in eating habits	15
Holiday	13
Christmas	12
Minor violation of the law	11

The total scores can be interpreted as follows:

Less than 150	30 per cent probability of developing an illness, i.e. no more than average risk
Between 150 and 300	50 per cent probability of developing an illness
Over 300	80 per cent probability of developing an illness

Figure 6.2 Holmes and Rahe stress scale based on life events

trivial event is seen as the end of the world, while at the other extreme, people manage to cope with apparently impossible situations. As the philosopher Epicititus said 'it is not how things are – it is how they seem.'

The role of personality

This brings us to another major aspect of stress, and one which has received particular attention in the context of coronary heart disease – personality. In the early twentieth century, when coronary heart disease was rare in comparison with today, the American doctor William Osler was still able to identify such a thing as the 'coronary-prone man', described as 'one who is keen and ambitious, the indicator of whose engines is set full speed ahead.'

This anticipated work done much later by the San Francisco cardiologists Friedman and Rosenman, who identified the 'Type A Personality' as being especially susceptible to coronary heart disease. Type A people are impatient, competitive and often critical of themselves and others. They:

- may be irritable or aggressive;
- may accentuate words in speech, even when special emphasis is not needed;
- move, eat and talk quickly;
- do not like waiting – they can't stand queues and may even try to hurry people through their sentences;
- tend to do two things at once;
- find it hard to relax;
- do not notice interesting or lovely things;
- tend to challenge other Type A people.

In contrast, Type B people are more easy going. They:

- are more patient and do not experience the same sense of urgency;
- do not feel a strong need to impress others;
- do not have 'free floating hostility';
- play games for relaxation and for fun – not to win;
- work calmly and without agitation;
- relax without feeling guilty.

In view of the significance of Type A and Type B behaviour, a number of questionnaires have been developed to help people come to a better awareness of their own personality, and potential risk from stress. One example is that developed by Dr Howard Glazer (see Figure 6.3).

The Glazer Stress Control Lifestyle Questionnaire
(Developed by Dr Howard I. Glazer)

Listed below are twenty pairs of adjectives or phrases separated by a series of boxes. Each pair represents two extremes. Each of us belongs somewhere along the line between the two extremes. For example, most of us are neither the most competitive nor the least competitive person we know. Tick the most appropriate box between the two extremes where you think you belong.

		1 2 3 4 5 6 7	
1	Doesn't mind leaving things temporarily unfinished	☐ ☐ ☐ ☐ ☐ ☐ ☐	Must get things finished once started
2	Calm and unhurried about appointments	☐ ☐ ☐ ☐ ☐ ☐ ☐	Never late for appointments
3	Not competitive	☐ ☐ ☐ ☐ ☐ ☐ ☐	Highly competitive
4	Listens well, lets others finish speaking	☐ ☐ ☐ ☐ ☐ ☐ ☐	Anticipates others in conversation
5	Never in a hurry, even when pressured	☐ ☐ ☐ ☐ ☐ ☐ ☐	Always in a hurry
6	Able to wait calmly	☐ ☐ ☐ ☐ ☐ ☐ ☐	Uneasy when waiting
7	Easy-going	☐ ☐ ☐ ☐ ☐ ☐ ☐	Always full speed ahead
8	Takes one thing at a time	☐ ☐ ☐ ☐ ☐ ☐ ☐	Tries to do more than one thing at a time, thinks about what to do next
9	Slow and deliberate in speech	☐ ☐ ☐ ☐ ☐ ☐ ☐	Vigorous and forceful in speech (uses a lot of gestures)
10	Concerned with satisfying him or herself, not others	☐ ☐ ☐ ☐ ☐ ☐ ☐	Wants recognition by others for a job well done
11	Slow doing things	☐ ☐ ☐ ☐ ☐ ☐ ☐	Fast doing things (eating, walking)
12	Easy-going	☐ ☐ ☐ ☐ ☐ ☐ ☐	Hard-driving
13	Expresses feelings openly	☐ ☐ ☐ ☐ ☐ ☐ ☐	Holds feelings in
14	Has a large number of interests	☐ ☐ ☐ ☐ ☐ ☐ ☐	Few interests outside work
15	Satisfied with job	☐ ☐ ☐ ☐ ☐ ☐ ☐	Ambitious, wants quick advancement on job

16	Never sets own deadlines	☐ ☐ ☐ ☐ ☐ ☐ ☐	Often sets own deadlines
17	Feels limited responsibility	☐ ☐ ☐ ☐ ☐ ☐ ☐	Always feels responsible
18	Never judges things in terms of numbers	☐ ☐ ☐ ☐ ☐ ☐ ☐	Often judges performance in terms of numbers (how many, how much)
19	Casual about work	☐ ☐ ☐ ☐ ☐ ☐ ☐	Takes work very seriously (works weekends, brings work home)
20	Not very precise	☐ ☐ ☐ ☐ ☐ ☐ ☐	Very precise (careful about details)

Total score: _____

What the score means

20–30	B2, relaxed and easy-going
30–59	Moderate Type B, coping well
60–79	Neither Type A nor Type B but a healthy AB
80–108	Moderate Type A or A2 who should be cautious
109–140	Extreme type A or A1, coronary-prone

Figure 6.3   The Glazer Stress Control Lifestyle Questionnaire

Obviously the link between stress and heart disease is not as clear-cut as this, but certainly individuals scoring over 100 should look at ways of changing their behaviour.

Stress and the workplace

There is a definite medical basis for believing that stress (in the sense of stress with which a person thinks is beyond his or her ability to cope) is bad for health. Clearly, to determine the stress level, both external and internal factors have to be looked at. The external factors include the pressures from outside the individual, whether these come from home, or work, or elsewhere. The most important internal factors are the individual's personality, and, tied in with this, their ability to cope.

But how big a problem is stress in the workplace? The answer to this question is inevitably coloured by the difficulties of definition and measurement mentioned at the start of this chapter. But while the exact extent of the problem cannot be quantified, what is clear is that we are looking at a potentially vast and expensive problem.

While some companies are recognising this and starting to act, many more are either unable or unwilling to accept that stress is a real issue. It is sadly still the case in many companies that people will not admit to being over stressed, feeling that this will be seen as inadequacy on their part and that the corporate attitude will be 'if you can't stand the heat, keep out of the kitchen'.

But awareness of the problem is growing. When in 1987 the CBI questioned employers about the reasons for absenteeism, it is significant that work-related stress was the third most frequently mentioned factor, after 'Poor motivation' and 'Family responsibilities' (CBI Report 'Managing for Attendance').

The cost of absenteeism is huge. In his Foreward to the Report referred to above, CBI Director General John Banham put the cost to the economy of employees who fail to turn up for work at over £5 billion every year. If stress is a significant part of this, as the Report suggests, it is clearly a major issue for employers.

It has been estimated that as many as 200 million days per year are lost from work by employees with stress-related illnesses such as headaches, depressions, anxiety and 'nervous debility'. If this is true, it means that in an average lifetime, the average employee is losing one and a half years' from work due to stress-related causes. This estimate probably attributes more absence to stress than is fair, but even so, there is no doubt that ill-health associated with stress is an expensive problem, and yet one to which many organisations will not admit.

Managers under stress

While the traditional image of the stressed person is the high-flying executive, dashing from meeting to meeting, stress can be found at every level of an organisation. Many managers feel that the pressure created by their work and the pace of change in their organisation are far greater than, say, ten years ago. Rapid change may bring with it feelings of insecurity, as will doubts about the company's profitability and future prospects.

Many senior managers lead a life which is physically very stressful and which offers few opportunities for rest and relaxation. Many have to travel long distances, and even if this is only within the UK, driving the company car on heavily-used motorways and other roads is stressful and unproductive. Some leading companies are now issuing guidelines recommending the use of public transport wherever practicable. Where cars are used, there are restrictions on the amount of driving time in any one day and recommendations as to rest breaks at regular intervals during a long drive.

But it is a myth that stress is just a problem for the busy executive. Supervisors often feel they have the worst of all worlds, with pressure from above to take on ever greater management responsibilities and pressure too from the people they are supervising.

Other employees

At shop floor level, people may feel that in the highly mechanised and computer controlled world of the modern factory, they have little control over their work, and little in which to take any sort of personal pride. This can in turn lead to a diminished feeling of self respect.

One of the reasons why Quality Circles have proved successful in many organisations is that they have given greater involvement and influence to the individual, who is able to see a value placed on his or her contribution. This in turn has led to a greater sense of involvement and commitment.

In one major chemical company which was planning a new manufacturing facility, operators were involved not only in planning physical things such as the layout of the control room, but also organisational issues such as the working of the shift system. As a result, the control room is a far better place to work – largely because of the the input made to its design by the people who would actually have to work in it – and the shift system works very well, even though it is so radical that management would never have dared propose it for fear of an instant walk-out.

The pressures of home and family must also be taken into account, for stress is by no means something which is restricted to the workplace. The home and the family can be very stressful in their own right, and apart from this, problems at home can deprive people of the essential support mechanisms which enable them to cope with a high level of pressure in other areas of their lives.

It is not at all surprising that the five life events at the top of the Holmes and Rahe stress scale (death of spouse, divorce, marital separation, jail term and death of a close family member) all involve a profound disruption of family life. At the same time, changes in society at large have meant that the close ties with the extended family which used to be taken for granted are now put in jeopardy by the fact that many people do not work in the area in which they were born, nor are they within easy reach of parents and other relations. Again, the effect of this can be to deprive people of support which would otherwise have helped them cope.

The good news is that, despite the complexity of the factors involved in stress, there are simple things that can be done to minimise the damage stress does. This is what the rest of this chapter deals with, both from the individual and the corporate standpoints.

Stress and the individual

We have already seen that there are many personal factors in stress, and at a simple level, what is stressful for one person may actually be a means of relaxation for another! Nevertheless, there are certain basic approaches which will help most people, and within this, we all need to work out for ourselves the things we find most helpful.

Awareness

As is the case with a number of other issues, the first step to coping is to increase awareness. We need to be more aware of what stress is and what stresses us. However, in some cases, this is easier said than done, for as we have already highlighted, one of the effects of stress is to cloud people's judgement, to the point at which not only their awareness of what is wrong, but also their ability to do anything about it, is prejudiced. It is precisely in this way that stress can become a downward spiral of greater pressure and despondency – leading ultimately to physical and mental illness.

Awareness of stress means not only being clear about what we find stressful (and here it may help to actually write down what our worries are) but also recognising the warning signs and accepting that stress is the cause. These can be divided into physical and mental warning signs (see Figure 6.4).

It must be emphasised that these may not necessarily be abnormal or indeed caused by stress at all. Often a pattern of unusual signs builds up, which goes beyond what is normal for that individual, and which cannot be put down to some other factor. In these cases we need to look at stress as a possible cause. Once we learn to recognise our own personal pattern, this gives us a useful early warning system for excessive stress in ourselves.

People often feel a huge sense of guilt about admitting that they are stressed, and indeed sometimes make matters worse by taking on an ever-increasing range of tasks and responsibilities as if they somehow had to prove to the rest of the world how well they can cope.

Physical effects:	Mental effects:
● palpitations (being aware of the beating of the heart)	● indecision
	● irritability
● chest pain	● anxiety
● indigestion	● over- or under-eating
● impotence	● tiredness
● tingling in arms and legs	● smoking
● neck and back pain	● drinking
● headaches and migraine	● accident-proneness
● skin rashes	
● double vision	
● lump in throat	

(Adapted from 'Work and Health' by Dr Andrew Melhuish)

Figure 6.4 – Physical and mental effects of stress

But there should be no shame attached to saying that you are suffering from stress – the number of hours in each day is after all finite – and if we are unable not only to recognise but also admit to stress, we are likely to find it very hard to do anything else which might help.

Getting the balance right

Once we know and accept that stress is a potential problem, probably the single most important next step is to ensure a proper balance in our lives. This balance needs to include not only work and family and all the other demands on our resources, but also time for ourselves, and opportunities for rest and relaxation. There needs to be balance at a day to day level. Just relaxing at weekends or on the annual holiday is not good enough – we need to have some time each day in which we stand back from the busy world and renew ourselves.

What we do with this time will vary from person to person – some will sit down with a book, some will get out for some exercise, some may even pray, or meditate, or do relaxation exercises. What matters is that we do have that time which we can call our own. In deciding how we spend it, we are then in a better position to decide how to plan the rest of our time, so that we are running our lives, rather than letting our lives run us.

For many managers, one of the most important parts of this is to give the right importance to work. Many managers spend most of their waking lives working, and so important is work to our sense of who we are that we tend to introduce ourselves to strangers in terms of where we work and what our position is. We are what we do.

There is little doubt that too much work – as with too much of anything else – is bad for you. We all know that all work and no play made Jack a dull boy, but what about Jack's dad, who drove 30,000 miles a year, usually put in a 70 hour working week with all the work he did in the evening and at weekends, and who died of a heart attack at the age of 44?

Although the UK is now a secular society, we are still dominated by the protestant work ethic which says that work is – in itself – a good thing. From this comes the far more questionable assumption that, as long as we are busy, we must be achieving something. Equally, there is a view that the longer we are at work, the more productive we must be. However, studies do show that effectiveness tails off rapidly at the end of a long working day – hence controls on the hours of work of lorry drivers, airline pilots and, most recently, hospital doctors.

For a healthy approach, we need to focus far more on outcomes, for it is what is achieved that counts, not the effort expended on the way. We may not be able to make changes on our own. We may need to spend more time with our managers and colleagues, exploring roles and responsibilities. We may find that training in priority-setting and time management techniques helps us achieve a better balance between the different calls on our time. But whatever we do, we must get the balance right.

Laughter

A life which is short on good humour may not only be unhappy, it may also be shorter as a result. There is a serious insight behind the famous *Reader's Digest* heading 'Laughter is the Best Medicine' and in classical times, Aristotle described laughter as 'a bodily exercise precious to health'.

Humour releases tension and is one of the best antidotes to stress. It can help smooth over conflicts and make work far more enjoyable. It can help us communicate better with each other and facilitate team-building, and when work is over, it helps us relax.

Exercise

Exercise has a key role in the promotion of good health, and lack of regular exercise is a significant risk factor for coronary heart disease. However, apart from any other benefit, exercise can help people cope more effectively with stress. Exercise helps people relax through changing the mental focus and being completely absorbing. People who exercise regularly say that worry about the impending deadline or a difficult meeting quickly evaporates as they exercise, also that the feelings of sheer exhilaration and physical well-being leave them better placed to cope with the pressures of life.

Perhaps one of the most dangerous aspects of stress is the anger and hostility we sometimes feel when we are under pressure, and again, people who do take regular exercise say that exercise is an excellent way of venting these powerful and potentially destructive feelings.

Exercise does not have to consist of running a mile every evening, or doing 40 lengths of the pool twice a week. Many people find that simply getting out in the fresh air for regular and reasonably brisk walks makes a big contribution to their general well-being and the reduction of stress.

Relaxation

We have seen that, when we are under stress, various changes take place in the body. These affect not only the heart, circulation and the way we breathe, but also the muscles – which tend to go tense in preparation for 'fight or flight'.

We do not have direct control over these changes – they take place under the control of the autonomic nervous system, which acts as a sort of autopilot to the body. Indeed, the changes may take us by surprise, as for example when we are sitting, frustrated, in an apparently unending traffic jam, and we suddenly realise that our knuckles have gone white because we are gripping the steering wheel so tightly.

We cannot simply switch off the autonomic nervous system in the way that an aircraft captain switches off the autopilot so as to resume manual operation of the aircraft's controls. But there are things we can do which reverse some of the body's physical reactions to stress, and at the same time release the mental tension.

For example, if we find we are breathing rapidly because we are about to go into a hostile meeting, consciously taking slow deep breaths will not only help reverse the body's physical response to stress, but will also make us feel more at peace mentally. Similarly, we can relax tense muscles by consciously tensing and then releasing them.

Some people find that meditation, yoga or self-hypnosis simultaneously helps them relax physically and achieve a spiritual peace which is a strong antidote to stress. Many people who will never do relaxation exercises regularly, or even dream of meditating, nevertheless take comfort from the awareness that there are things they can do if the feelings of pressure become intolerable. This contributes to the perception that they are in control of their lives – and not the other way round – which, as mentioned above, is fundamental to combating stress in general.

Organisation and efficiency

Better time management is not a complete answer to workload problems, because there will always come a point where we simply cannot do all the things either we or others would like us to do. However, many managers are not as well-organised as they might be, and for these, improved time management can claw back valuable chunks of time and help them find a way through a seemingly impossible workload.

In this context, efficiency does not mean standing over ourselves with a stop-watch and a clipboard, it means simply getting value for money out of our time. People achieve the same ends in different ways, so there is no one work pattern which will work for everybody. However, many managers report the following principles as helpful ones:

- be realistic about how long things take, and allow some time in each day and each week to deal with unforeseeable (or unforeseen) demands on your time;
- don't work from day to day – plan ahead;
- if you can't deliver, don't promise;
- involve others in what you are doing, and delegate effectively;
- regularly review what you've got to do;
- focus on quality rather than quantity – better a one page report in which every word counts than a 10 page one which explores the issues but never comes to the point;
- never write anything, call anyone or go to any meeting without a clear outcome in mind. You may have to adapt your thoughts as you go along, but if you start off with a clear idea, you are less likely to waste your time, and other people's;
- prioritise for yourself and for your staff, distinguishing between urgency and importance.

Managers can do much to help the people who work for them by making sure that jobs are structured in order to create a mix of tasks, and that the right person is put in the job. In addition, attention to all aspects of the working environment – heating, lighting, noise, ergonomics, decoration – will help reduce stress.

Communication

Much stress in organisations could be reduced by better communication. A full treatment of this topic is outside the scope of this book, but what must be emphasised here is the importance of good communication, both for our own stress level and for that of others.

In our dealings with others, we should always try to be courteous, regardless of how we feel. But this does not mean suppressing strong feelings, such as anger and disappointment. Indeed, to do so can be extremely destructive. Many people find that the best way to deal with these feelings is to express them – not in a burst of temper, but simply by saying how they feel.

Be your own best friend

Many problems of relationships and communication – in work as well as outside – stem from poor self esteem. If we have little self-respect, we may be driven to take on virtually impossible workloads in order to receive the approval of those we work with, and probably end up by disappointing them into the bargain and making matters worse.

Most of us want others to think well of us, and yet sometimes we are our own worst enemies, seeing life in terms of a string of problems which will only expose our own inadequacies to the world at large. We dare not dream of success in case that somehow tempts fate, and often by fearing the worst, we make the worst more likely – the self-fulfilling prophecy.

We all have skills to offer, we all have potential to be more tomorrow than we are today, and we need to realise that, to a great extent, we create our own destiny. So the final point in this section about stress from the personal point of view is this: to avoid stress, we need to be at peace with ourselves.

Stress and the organisation

Stress is not just an issue for individuals, it is one that requires a positive response from managers. In assessing and managing stress within the organisation, the following 11 principles should help as the basis of a practical approach:

1. Physical and environmental sources of stress, such as noise, fumes, poor lighting, unergonomic machinery etc. must be investigated and dealt with.

These factors are direct causes of stress, but they may also contribute indirectly, e.g. through people being demotivated because of the poor quality of the working environment and the feeling they have no control over the conditions in which they work. The perception that 'no one cares what we have to put up with' is stressful in itself.

2. Managers should be encouraged to recognise and acknowledge the signs of stress in themselves and others.

This implies both acceptance by senior managers that stress is a real issue, and some form of training so that the signs of stress can be identified and acted upon.

3. Positive values such as empathy, supportiveness and encouragement should be promoted, as opposed to negative ones such as aggression, ruthlessness and win-at-all-costs.

Again, this is very much a question of the overall culture of the organisation, which will be determined by a number of factors, one of the most important being the leadership and example given by senior managers.

4. There should be a clear style of management. Responsibilities should be as well-defined as possible, so that people know where they stand and what is expected of them.

We have seen that one of the principal themes within the field of stress is change and in particular, people's ability to cope with it. A common perception among middle managers is that 'the goal posts are always moving'. Not only may this be stressful in itself, but it prevents people achieving their full potential – because they do not really understand the standard they are expected to achieve.

5. People must be given the resources and power to achieve what is expected of them.

Accountability without control is intrinsically stressful.

6. The style of management should be consistent. Managers need to be able to cope with change, but if they receive conflicting or even contradictory messages – e.g. about priorities – stress and friction are almost inevitable.

7. Appraisal and career development procedures must allow people to reach their full potential.

People tend to associate stress with jobs which demand too much rather than too little, but this is misleading, for work which does not properly engage a person's talents and skills can be stressful too.

8. The use of outside counselling agencies to help support people with stress problems should be investigated.

The setting up of Employee Assistance Programmes (EAPs) is an approach which has proved successful in the USA and one which is attracting increasing attention in the UK. The use of an outside body to provide this service offers three particular benefits – specialist expertise, objectivity and confidentiality for the individual being counselled.

9. People should be involved as fully as possible in decisions which affect them.

As noted above, the feeling of powerlessness is a major source of stress in an organisation in which the management style does not give people much say in decisions which have implications for them.

10. People should be allowed as much control over their work as possible.

Effective delegation is a major tool not only in combating stress, but also in making the best use of people, time and other resources.

11. The cost to the organisation of stress-related absence should be investigated.

Although it is difficult to quantify the absence which is specifically due to stress, knowing as much as possible about the financial scale of the problem provides a powerful incentive for managers at all levels to implement action on stress.

- Is stress a problem in our organisation?
- Have managers received any training to enable them to identify and deal with stress in themselves and in others?
- Have physical causes of stress been dealt with?
- Does the organisational culture prize positive or negative values?
- Is there a clear and consistent style of management?
- Are people given the resources they need to meet their responsibilities, and to develop their full potential?
- Has the use of outside counselling agencies been investigated?
- Are people fully involved in decisions which affect them?
- How good are our corporate communications?
- Are people given help to make the best use of their time and other resources?

CHAPTER 7
Alcohol

The pleasures of alcohol contrast sharply with the health problems caused by excessive consumption. Alcohol related risks include liver damage, cancer, accidents, and violence. This is a real issue for employers who lose more than £1.5 billion each year from lost production resulting from alcohol abuse.

Control of alcohol consumption is generally based on drinking within 'sensible limits', not total abstinence. There is wide acceptance of safe limits for men and for women, which specify weekly consumption on the basis of standard units of alcohol. Motivation to reduce drinking requires awareness of potential health effects, and knowledge of practical measures which can help maintain drinking at lower levels.

The employer has a vital role to play in reducing the damage caused by alcohol. Effective measures include education for employees in the health risks of excessive drinking, training for managers to identify early warning signs of alcohol abuse, and the formulation of clear policies which ensure fair and consistent treatment of those with alcohol related problems.

Alcohol is an integral part of our culture, and has been for a long time. There is evidence of the use of alcohol in most of the early civilisations, and the Egyptians were using it for medicinal purposes 4000 years ago. It seems always to have been a mixed blessing, with concern about drunkenness resulting in many attempts at restriction – including punishment by death. Today, the pleasures and the problems of alcohol are as polarised as ever. Alcohol consumption is running at an extremely high level, and the appreciation of good alcohol – from fine wine to real ale – is an important leisure activity. On the other hand, concerns about the hazards of alcohol now go beyond drunkenness and include a large number of chronic health effects. Other major problems include alcohol's influence on social and family behaviour, its contribution to accidents, and its effect on work.

Facts and figures

Alcohol consumption in Great Britain has been rising steadily for 50 years. From 1960 to 1981, the average consumption per individual of beer rose by more than 50 per cent, of spirits by 200 per cent, and of wine by 500 per cent. In 1989, the average consumption of alcohol by adults in England and Wales was equivalent to 9.3 litres of pure alcohol per head. This equates to about 450 pints of beer or 30 bottles of whisky for every man and woman in the country.

Expenditure on alcohol is staggering. The 1985 average figures are:

£326 per person in Scotland;
£277 per person in England;
£264 per person in Wales;
£209 per person in Northern Ireland.

More money is spent on alcohol than on clothes, and alcohol accounts for the equivalent of half of all consumer spending on food. This amounts to about £13,000,000,000 per year – some half of which goes to government tax revenue. Attempts to quantify the costs of alcohol-related problems are limited, and cannot include a measure for human suffering, but show a substantial problem. The following figures summarise estimates made by Alcohol Concern using 1986 data from England and Wales.

Industry cost (loss of production, etc.)	£1,650 million
NHS cost (hospital treatment, etc.)	£116 million
Health education and research	£1 million
Traffic accidents	£107 million
Criminal activities	£39 million

Amounting to a total of over £1,900 million.

An indication of the human side is given by various published estimates suggesting that alcohol is associated with:

- 88 per cent of criminal damage;
- 78 per cent of assault;
- 65 per cent of serious head injuries;
- 60 per cent of attempted suicide;
- 35 per cent of road accidents;
- 30 per cent of divorces;

- 40 per cent of domestic violence;
- 35 per cent of child abuse.

Although drinking is widespread amongst both sexes and all adult age ranges, professions and social classes, it does show some distinct biases.

Sex

Heavy drinking is predominantly a male activity, with men drinking four times more alcohol than women. However there is evidence that alcohol consumption is currently rising much more sharply amongst women than men.

Age

The highest drinking age group is that of young adults aged 18 to 24. As age increases, alcohol consumption steadily declines and those aged 65 and over drink, on average, about a quarter of the young adults' level. There is only limited information about drinking before the age of 18. Although it is accepted that laws on under age drinking are widely flouted, studies in Scotland and England have suggested that drinking among the majority of adolescents is not a major or increasing problem, and that such drinking is not an accurate predictor of later difficulties in adulthood.

Profession

Not surprisingly, the occupations with the highest drinking levels tend to be those with everyday access to alcohol such as publicans, hotel employees, restaurateurs, etc. Other high consumption professions are often those where business entertaining and socialising are common, and include journalists, insurance brokers, and medical practitioners.

Social status

The social class gradient for drinking is the reverse of that for smoking, with the highest drinking being in professional and self employed groups (95 per cent drinkers), and the lowest in blue collar occupations (88 per cent drinkers).

In addressing health issues associated with drinking, it is worth noting that there is often a marked discrepancy between the amount people drink, and the amount they *think* they drink. This is illustrated by some figures from a Department of Health survey which considered drinking self-image. The following table shows the drinking classification given of themselves by 18 to 24 year old drinkers whose drinking was actually 'high' (the equivalent of 18 to 25 pints of beer per week)

hardly drink at all	2 per cent
drink a little	4 per cent
drink a moderate amount	71 per cent
drink quite a lot	21 per cent
drink heavily	1 per cent

Alcohol units

Although the concentration of alcohol in different drinks varies widely, the actual amount of alcohol in most 'glasses' of drink is much the same – about 8 grams. This has created the convenient concept of the 'standard drink' or 'unit'. Thus, a unit of alcohol is equivalent to a half-pint of beer or lager, a standard glass of wine, or a measure of spirits. Figure 7.1 gives more details of the units of alcohol in common drinks.

Drink	Units
Ordinary beer, lager or cider	
half pint	1
one pint	2
one can (440 ml)	1.5
Strong beer, lager or cider	
half pint	2
one pint	4
one can	3
Spirits	
one standard measure	1
one bottle	30
Wine	
one standard glass	1
one bottle	7
one litre bottle	10
Sherry	
one standard small measure	1
one bottle	13

Figure 7.1 Units of alcohol in common drinks

LOOKING AFTER CORPORATE HEALTH

Effects of alcohol on health

Before presenting the long list of damaging health effects which can result from alcohol consumption, it should be stressed that the vast majority of people who drink alcohol appear to do so with no damage to their health whatever. However, it is clear from the above statistics that *excessive* drinking creates some enormous problems, that the majority of people who drink to excess are employed, and that it would be impossible to have a comprehensive corporate health programme which did not address the issue of alcohol consumption. The effects of alcohol will now be considered under the main categories in which problems are likely to occur.

Alcohol and accidents

Between one and three drinks, depending on sex and body weight, will cause the level of alcohol in the blood to rise to 50 milligrams per 100 millilitres of blood. At this level the individual feels relaxed and happy, and is able to socialise more easily. However, judgement is also impaired, driving can start to become reckless, and accidents are more likely. After four units of alcohol, most people will reach the legal limit for driving in Great Britain, of 80 mg/100ml. At this level people are losing their inhibitions and becoming talkative. They are also twice as likely to have a road accident if they drive – but even if they are cyclists or pedestrians, they are more likely to have an accident resulting in injury. More than half of hospital admissions for head injuries in Glasgow were found to be over the alcohol legal limit for driving. At about seven units of alcohol, the blood concentration will reach 150 mg/100ml. Speech is slurred, and the risk of a motor accident becomes ten times that when sober. At nine to ten units the blood level reaches 200 mg/100ml. The individual may stagger when trying to walk, and is twenty times more likely to have a road accident.

Alcohol also increases the likelihood of injury resulting from personal violence. Domestic violence, violent crime, hooliganism, pub fights, etc., have all been linked with alcohol, though alcohol is rarely, if ever, the single cause.

The information on road accidents is the most studied aspect of the link between alcohol and accidents. However, it would be quite reasonable to assume the same connection with workplace accidents. Health and Safety Executive publications stress that workplace drinking presents an increased risk of serious injury to both the drinker and others. This is particularly the case when good judgement or reaction times are necessary, and when dangerous machinery is involved. Examples are fork lift truck driving, and crane operation.

Alcohol and productivity

Even if an individual does not have a potentially dangerous job, lunch-time drinking still has a significant effect on afternoon work performance. Keyboard operators, for example, may have an increased error rate after only one unit of alcohol. Managers may have their judgement affected, and salespeople and other customer contact staff may make remarks that they would not usually make. These effects can also follow a heavy drinking session the night before.

Alcohol and the liver

Alcohol consumption is known to be strongly related to the risk of developing cirrhosis of the liver. This risk is significantly higher than normal for men drinking 5 units of alcohol per day, and women drinking 3 units per day. All alcohol drunk passes into the blood stream and is transported to the liver. The first effect of sustained drinking on the liver is the deposition of excess fat within the liver cells. This results in a condition known as 'fatty liver' – not harmful in itself since, although the liver is enlarged, the essential liver functions continue fairly normally. However, if drinking continues, inflammation of the liver may develop, and the condition becomes alcoholic hepatitis. Liver cells are killed, and the essential functions of the liver are impaired. If severe, alcoholic hepatitis is extremely serious, often resulting in death from jaundice, liver coma, kidney failure, or uncontrollable infection. There is little effective treatment, and the main hope is that sufficient liver cells survive to enable recovery of liver function when alcohol consumption is completely stopped.

Cirrhosis is a chronic disease which may follow alcoholic hepatitis, or occur independently. In cirrhosis, liver cells are killed and permanently replaced with fibrous tissue – often called 'scar tissue'. Eventually the whole liver is criss-crossed with a network of fine scars causing distortion and contraction of the organ. The extent to which the liver can continue its proper functions depends upon the amount of damage, but is dependent upon future abstinence from alcohol.

Alcohol and the brain

Alcohol is a common cause of mental illness. This results firstly from the toxic effect of contact between alcohol in the blood and the tissues of the brain and nervous system, and secondly from the social damage which may be caused by alcohol dependency. The first group of effects may be shown as 'alcoholic dementia'. This is an irreversible intellectual deterioration similar to senile dementia. The patient may show depression or indifference, but will also have suffered significant loss of mental powers, including impairment of memory, comprehension and judgement. Some sufferers exhibit Korsakoff's syndrome – named after the nineteenth century Russian neurologist – in which there is an attempt to cover the loss of memory with stories of non-existent experiences. Deprivation of alcohol causes withdrawal symptoms – tremors, confusion, and visual hallucinations – and the sufferer is likely to go to considerable lengths to keep drinking, whilst denying excessive drinking. A brain scan will show atrophy of the brain cortex – the outer layer, or 'grey matter' – concerned with the higher functions of the nervous system.

Other effects of alcohol on the brain include 'Wernicke's encephalopathy' which, like Korsakoff's syndrome, results from deficiency of vitamin B1 (thiamine). Symptoms include paralysis of eye movement, loss of balance, and extreme confusion. Drinking often results in memory blackouts – not necessarily a sign of irreversible damage, but a clear warning signal. 'Delirium tremens' is a frightening withdrawal symptom, sometimes resulting in death from heart failure. Vivid hallucinations are associated with feelings of terror and distortion of time.

Alcohol and the pancreas

Alcohol can be the cause of a condition known as acute pancreatitis, producing severe abdominal pain and vomiting. Continued alcohol abuse can lead to chronic pancreatitis, in which the pancreas (a gland near the stomach) becomes filled with chalky cysts. Because the pancreas is the body's source of insulin, damage is likely to result in diabetes. Other problems may arise, including narrowing or blockage of the bowel. Pancreatitis is most common in men aged 30 to 45 who drink 15 to 20 units of alcohol per day, and also have a diet rich in fat and protein. Mortality is high amongst those who develop pancreatitis and then go on drinking.

Alcohol and the heart

Discussion about heart disease risk factors in Chapter 3, showed that alcohol is *not* one of the main risk factors for coronary heart disease although alcohol can certainly affect other conditions, such as blood pressure, which *are* risk factors. However, sustained drinking over a period of years does cause damage to the heart, both by the direct toxic effect of alcohol on the heart muscle (cardiomyopathy), and by nutritional deficiency common in people who obtain their calories from alcohol but do not eat properly. Heart disease caused by alcohol results in breathlessness together with obvious heart palpitations – there is usually none of the acute pain associated with angina. If the condition progresses, fluid in the chest and swelling of the ankles develops from failure of the heart to maintain adequate circulation. Pulse rate rises, the heartbeat becomes irregular, and death may result from heart failure. Fortunately this disease can be reversed, even at quite an advanced stage, provided the individual gives up alcohol completely.

Alcohol and cancer

Alcohol contributes to the development of cancer in a number of ways. Cancer of the throat is an increased risk for drinkers consuming ten units or more of alcohol per day. Heavy drinking increases the risks of cancer of the mouth threefold, of the larynx fourfold, and of the oesophagus twofold. Liver cell cancer is also associated with drinking, as a complication of cirrhosis. Up to 10 per cent of those with alcoholic cirrhosis go on to develop liver cancer. There is also some evidence that heavy drinking in women increases the risk of breast cancer, perhaps as much as doubling the risk.

Alcohol and pregnancy

Much recent publicity has been given to the risks to unborn children, resulting from drinking in pregnancy. More research findings are awaited on this subject, and it seems likely that other factors such as diet will also play a part. However, drinking in pregnancy can certainly contribute to permanent damage including facial abnormalities, low weight, and mental retardation. There is also an increased risk of spontaneous abortion. The risk seems greatest in the early stages of pregnancy, and it is sensible for women who are in early pregnancy, or who are planning to become pregnant, to minimise their drinking.

Alcoholism

In developing company alcohol procedures and policies, it is possible to get side-tracked by the term 'alcoholic'. In other words to attempt to devise special approaches for people with this disease. So what is an alcoholic? The fact is that there is a grey dividing line which separates those with a drinking 'problem' from those who could be classified as alcoholics. Definitions of alcoholism include compulsion to take alcohol on a continuous or periodic basis, both to experience its effects and to avoid the unpleasantness of its absence – alcoholics are addicted

　　　　　　　　　　　　　LOOKING AFTER CORPORATE HEALTH

to alcohol. The term alcoholism is now somewhat unfashionable, with 'alcohol dependence' more commonly used, but is in any case of questionable value in formulating policies. You do not have to be dependent on alcohol to suffer health effects from its use, and health education specialists generally agree that there is more to be gained by directing efforts towards the less heavy drinkers – because there are more of them. An idea of the numbers involved comes from Office of Health Economics estimates that 0.4 per cent of the population, some 150,000 people have alcohol dependence. On the other hand 2 per cent, or 700,000 people have 'problem drinking' which results in harm to themselves or others, and 8 per cent, or 3 million people have sufficiently heavy drinking for this to cause acute intoxication which could result in accidents or social problems.

How much is too much?

The effects of alcohol at different levels of consumption have already been considered, and are illustrated in Figure 7.2. Although it is recognised that the effects of alcohol can differ considerably from person to person, there is considerable attraction in the simplicity of advisory limits which can be applied to virtually everyone. Such guidelines were suggested by the Royal College of Psychiatrists, and have become widely accepted. The most used figures in their guidelines are those which set the levels for low risk drinking. These are:

FOR MEN, less than 21 units per week
FOR WOMEN, less than 14 units per week

In fact, the guidelines give three levels of drinking – 'harmful', 'increased risk', and 'low risk'. The levels are as follows:

	units of alcohol per week	
	Men	*Women*
Harmful drinking	*50 or more*	*35 or more*
Increased risk drinking	*21 to 49*	*14 to 34*
Low risk drinking	*less than 21*	*less than 14*

One question which has caused much discussion is – 'is there a level of drinking which is actually good for you?' This resulted from the publication of the so-called 'U-shaped curve' which showed that those people who do not drink at all appear to have a slightly higher risk of dying from heart disease than those who drink moderately (about one

Blood alcohol concentration (mg per 100 ml blood)	Effect
40	feel relaxed, increased accident risk
60	feel cheerful, judgement impaired
80	feeling of well-being, loss of inhibitions, slow reaction time
120	talkative and excited, emotional and impulsive
150	silly and confused, slurred speech, may be aggressive
200	Staggering, drunk, double vision
300–400	unconscious
500–600	dead

Figure 7.2 Effects of alcohol at different blood concentrations

unit per day). Further studies have shown that the non-drinkers include people who have had to give up drinking because of poor health, and that this may be the cause of that group's apparently higher mortality rate. However, the debate continues – monitored keenly by moderate drinkers.

Alcohol and work

From the information presented so far, it will be clear that alcohol has an effect on work. Alcohol is drunk predominantly by working people, and it affects their health, their mental state, and their risk of accidents and death. The costs to society resulting from alcohol are headed by the cost to businesses of lost production, accident damage, etc. It is unlikely that current costings cover the full scale of the problem, but conservative estimates show costs to business of the order of £1.5 billion, of which the major components are sickness absence, and lost resource through premature death.

In preparing alcohol policies, it is useful to itemise the ways in which drinking can become a workplace issue:

1. Alcohol related illness, together with hangovers, results in high levels of absenteeism.

2. Those who work under the influence of alcohol are less productive than those who are sober.
3. Employees who have to use decision-making and judgement skills, such as managers, will be less effective after drinking.
4. Alcohol significantly increases the risk of accidents, both to the drinker and to others at work.
5. Drinkers can be the cause of disruption and social friction at work, and can be difficult to manage.
6. Heavy drinkers often have domestic and/or financial problems which prevent them from concentrating fully on their work.

Action against alcohol abuse

So how are the damaging effects of alcohol prevented? And what can companies do to help? For those who drink, but at moderate levels and without problems, the only requirement is to keep it that way. This is *not* guaranteed. Alcohol dependency generally takes 10 to 15 years to develop, and is a risk for about one in 25 drinkers. All drinkers need to know the risks, and need to be alert to the early warning signs of dependency. They also need to know when they are most vulnerable, since alcohol dependency is usually related to other problems – such as work or marital stress. Employers have a vital role here. They present far and away the greatest educational opportunity for most adults, and alcohol awareness is an essential component of the corporate healthcare plan.

For those who drink, and *do* have a problem, taking action has five key stages:

1. Acknowledging the problem.
2. Wanting to cut down (or stop).
3. Commitment to an action programme.
4. Finding help and support.
5. Monitoring progress.

Acknowledgement that there is an alcohol problem is not necessarily easy. What is self-evident to friends and family may be strenuously denied by the individual. The wide acceptance of standard alcohol units and 'sensible' limits has been extremely helpful here since it enables, indeed obliges, us to compare our drinking levels with those of others. However, for those who are already substantially alcohol dependent, acknowledgement of a problem may require some precipitating event. In talking to people who have tackled a drinking problem, it is notable how consistently they point to some occurrence which suddenly made them realise they had to take action. The occurrence may have been deeply distressing – perhaps involving violence, illness, or trouble with the law. A corporate health plan, with a commitment to being preventive rather than reactive, has a great part to play here – perhaps by creating the turning point event before others are harmed. We will later consider ways in which this might be achieved at work.

A desire to stop drinking – the second action stage – is not the same as recognising the problem. Many people know themselves to be drinking excessively, but have no intention of cutting down. This may be because they choose to accept the health risks – or fail to appreciate their magnitude. It may also be because alcohol is being used to block out some problem in the individual's life, and the problem of alcohol dependency is less than that of confronting the personal issues. These issues may need real support and help to be tackled in their own right – and hectoring about excessive drinking may hinder rather than help at this stage. This requires sympathetic understanding from those providing help, who need to know that alcohol may be providing:

- escape from family problems, work pressures, etc.;
- alternatives to personal relationships, success, etc.;
- courage to face fears and lack of confidence;
- avoidance of failure, inadequacy, loneliness, etc.

The role of employers here is invaluable, if they are willing to provide the necessary counselling and support. This together with assistance from workplace friends and colleagues, is likely to make work much the best place for achieving real results.

The desire to change must now be backed up with an absolutely clear action programme. This must establish targets which can be achieved and measured, and must specify just how the reduction in drinking is to be achieved. The targets need to be set with reference to the information on 'safe' levels earlier in the chapter. There are two obvious alternative targets. The first is to give up alcohol altogether. For many people this is a more satisfactory target than merely to attempt to cut down. It has a satisfying feeling of achievement about it, and there will be no ambiguity about whether it has been accomplished or not. For some people, this is their only real option anyway. These include those with cirrhosis of the liver, for whom continued drinking is a real risk to life. The actions are relatively straightforward – no buying or accepting drinks. Here again though, support from work is needed. This is a drinking culture and it is important that no-one is pressurised to drink when they don't want to. If drink is ever provided at work, then non-alcoholic alternatives should always be available. Those choosing this course of action need to know that they are not alone. About ten per cent of the adult population do not drink at all.

The second obvious target – likely to be chosen by the majority – is to settle for the recommended limits. In other words, 21 units per week for men, and 14 units per week for women. This is less straightforward because it involves more careful monitoring. It also needs some supplementary 'rules', for example:

- the weekly limit should not be consumed at one session! (alcohol is likely to do more harm when consumed in binges, and should ideally be reasonably spread over the week);
- there should be severe limits if dangerous machinery is to be used, or if driving;
- there must be accurate monitoring of the units consumed – especially when drinks are poured at home.

Taking this approach can be far from easy, especially if it involves a substantial reduction and the individual's social life involves many opportunities for drinking. However, the many people who have trodden this path before, have left much advice about ways in which the difficulties can be minimised. It might be useful to summarise the expert tips which have accumulated:

- be occupied – do other things as well as drinking, such as talking, playing games, etc.;
- savour the taste – drink for the flavour rather than the effect;
- take small sips – pace the drinking by deliberately slowing the rate at which you finish a glass;
- beware of rounds – avoid the trap of getting involved in large rounds where everyone is obliged to buy drink. Don't buy alcohol for yourself in your round;
- use low alcohol options – there are now low alcohol versions of most common drinks, in fact it is the fastest growing sector of the drinks trade;
- change your drink – old drinks are associated with old habits. New limits may be easier to achieve with a new drink, especially if it has a lower alcohol concentration;
- use the money saved – enormous amounts of money are spent on alcohol, and it can be extremely motivating to use the money saved for some desired project.

The next stage in the programme is that of finding help and support, and several references have already been made to the important role here for the employer. This will also be covered in the final section of the chapter. All lifestyle changes are easier with moral support, and friends and family can make the difference between success and failure. The supporter needs to be genuinely enthusiastic – but should not take a policing role. The responsibility for change lies with the individual in question, and any feeling that the responsibility can be transferred to someone else reduces the likelihood of success. The feeling to cultivate is that of personal honour being at stake – a commitment to oneself which simply must not be broken. However, maintaining that strength of mind is much easier with encouragement and this is a vital part of the role played by organisations such as Alcoholics Anonymous, and Alcohol Concern, who are ready to help at any time.

Finally, the plan needs to include progress monitoring. The suggestion above that the money saved is put to a tangible purpose is one good way of marking progress, as well as being highly motivating. Other ways are to set dates to review progress – perhaps to take stock each month, and to keep a drinking record in a diary or notebook, so that the weekly intake can be carefully monitored.

What can employers do?

Throughout this chapter it has been suggested that dealing with the health hazards of alcohol should be a feature of corporate healthcare programmes, and that the employer is uniquely placed to make a real contribution to dealing with this health issue. In practice, the employer's response can be considered in four areas:

1. Education of the workforce.
2. Education of management.
3. Locating and helping problem drinkers.
4. Development of an alcohol policy.

Educating the workforce

The general approach to health education is reviewed in Chapter 10. Alcohol is a natural subject for inclusion in workplace education programmes, firstly because it is relevant to the majority of working people, second because it has direct effects on work, and third because it is a *chronic* health problem – with slow effects which might be overlooked unless someone else points them out. One particular point, relevant to all education but especially important here, is that the message must *not* be boring. Academic lectures are unlikely to provoke action from the sorts of people most vulnerable, and a reasonably direct, campaigning approach is probably most effective. The subject lends itself well to quizzes, demonstrations, etc, and there are useful posters and booklets to support the message – the Health Education Authority, and the Scottish Health Education Board have particularly striking material on this subject. Topics to be covered in health education include:

- the meaning of alcohol units, safe drinking limits, and the alcohol content of common drinks;
- the health effects of alcohol;
- the accident risks after drinking;
- the social and family problems related to excessive drinking;
- early warning signs of alcohol dependency;
- methods of reducing alcohol consumption.

Educating management

The approach of many managers to alcohol problems amongst their staff is to ignore the signs until the problems become intolerable, and then to take dramatic action such as dismissal. This will have helped neither the individual nor the company, and we later suggest company alcohol policies which prevent this extreme reaction. However, to implement more considered policies, managers themselves will need training, with particular emphasis on the following areas:

- identifying the early warning signs of alcohol dependency in employees (these include lateness and absenteeism, the smell of alcohol, deterioration in personal appearance, conflict with colleagues, and poor concentration);
- working with employees to find the underlying causes of alcohol problems;
- counselling skills to aid employees in tackling excessive drinking;
- company procedures for responding to alcohol dependent employees, how to help, and when to use disciplinary procedures;
- sources of additional help and support (inside and outside the organisation).

Managers can also set a good example by not drinking at lunchtime themselves, and not providing alcoholic drinks routinely at meetings. The impression given by providing cheap alcohol in staff clubs and bars is also to be avoided.

Finding and helping problem drinkers

Organisations which offer help to employees with drinking problems

---

are facing up to one of today's major health hazards, and taking steps to safeguard their main resource – their people. However, they can also face criticism. This often comes from other employees who feel that while they are expected to be punctual and productive, those who are foolish enough to drink too much are treated with kid gloves and allowed time off. Help for drinkers must therefore follow clearly stated policy guidelines which are the same for everyone – and which must be clearly explained to everyone. In essence, alcohol problems should be treated in the same way as any other health problem affecting an employee.

Providing help requires recognition of problem drinking at the earliest possible stage. This is part of the reason for emphasising the education of management in recognising early warning signs. However, in the hope of making this foolproof, it is often asked whether alcohol dependency can be detected by a health screening programme. The answer is – not with certainty. Two screening tests are a possibility. The first would be to measure alcohol directly in blood, urine, or breath. However, a negative result could be guaranteed simply by abstaining for a period before the test. So unless the screening was undertaken either randomly or extremely frequently, both of which would be impractical for most organisations, this approach would not confirm an individual's drink problem. The second test was mentioned in Chapter 3. It is the blood test for gamma-glutamyltransferase (GGT). This test can now be undertaken quickly and easily with a desk-top blood analyser. Strictly speaking, this is really a test for liver damage, although the majority of cases will have resulted from alcohol abuse. GGT testing can be a useful screen, and can give valuable warning to drinkers who are beginning to suffer health damage. But it is *not* a definitive test for alcoholism. The majority of people who drink too much would have a perfectly acceptable GGT result, and a positive GGT result could have causes other than alcohol. In practice, the most effective alcohol screening uses questionnaires, which look for drinking problems with questions like:

- do you ever feel guilty about your drinking?
- do you drink in the morning?
- do you feel you should cut down?
- do other people criticise your drinking?

These questionnaires are very effective as part of the health education programme, and may help to demonstrate to a drinker that there is a problem. However, unless there is a guarantee of absolute confidentiality, those with the greatest problems will simply give false answers.

In reality, then, there is no real substitute for relying on the sensitivity of managers to identify problem drinkers, and in encouraging drinkers to ask for help without fear of punishment.

Alcohol policies

We have already suggested a number of policy approaches to dealing with alcohol. To be effective, these need to be drawn together and presented as a written, formal policy. The policy should be properly authorised, and made available to the whole workforce. A number of organisations, including the CBI, the Health Education Authority, and the Health and Safety Executive, have published guidance on policy content, and the following notes itemise the main issues to be addressed:

1. The objective of the policy should be declared as assisting employees who are problem drinkers, in the interests of health and safety, by setting out the organisation's intentions regarding confidentiality, job security, sickness benefit, pension rights, and disciplinary procedures.
2. Since problem drinkers are found at all employment levels, the policy should apply independently of status.
3. The organisation should make every effort to ensure that an employee with a drink problem will be given advice and other help. Time off work will be allowed if necessary, and employment will be protected. Advice and help can be provided in-house where there are suitable facilities and staff. Otherwise, outside help will be arranged with specialist agencies or general practitioners.
4. An employee whose problem has come to light as a result of poor performance, absenteeism, or accidents, should have the opportunity to discuss the problem and be offered help.
5. Employees who believe they have a drink problem should be encouraged to seek help, and be advised where this can be obtained.
6. If problems are diagnosed as alcohol related, the employee should have the same protection of employment and pension rights, as would be the case with any other form of ill health.
7. If an offer of help or diagnosis is refused, this should not of itself be grounds for disciplinary action. However, unacceptable behaviour or work would then be subject to normal disciplinary procedures.

8. Should alcohol related problems recur following help or treatment, the situation should be reviewed sympathetically and further help considered, though not guaranteed.
9. All treatment records should remain strictly confidential.
10. Employees should be entitled to representation by their union at any stage in the procedures.
11. The policy should come under the authority of an identified senior person in the organisation, delegated on a day-to-day basis to line managers.

The following questions will act as a guide to the actions necessary to introduce an effective alcohol programme and policy into the workplace:

- Do we ever make alcohol available at work? If so, could it be restricted? Are non-alcoholic alternatives always provided?
- Have we ever given employees information or training, explaining the health risks of alcohol, and the 'safe drinking levels'?
- Have managers received training on the early identification of alcohol problems at work, and on the approach to take to problem drinkers among their staff?
- Do we provide help to employees who have a drinking problem?
- Do all employees know exactly what to do and who to approach, if they believe that they or a colleague have a drinking problem and need help?
- Do all employees know that any action or treatment relating to alcohol abuse will be treated in the strictest confidence?
- Do we have a clear written policy, setting out the help provided for problem drinkers, the protection of employment, and the use of disciplinary procedures?
- Does the policy make it clear that all levels of employee will be treated equally with regard to problem drinking?
- Is the company policy on alcohol freely available to all employees?
- Are the policies and procedures relating to alcohol, the clear responsibility of a named senior manager or director?

CHAPTER 8
Smoking

Smoking – and especially cigarette smoking – is bad for our health. So significant is it – as one of the major risk factors for coronary heart disease, and as the major risk factor for lung cancer and bronchitis – that public health programmes in both the USA and the UK place 'stopping people smoking' at the head of their action lists.

In spite of the addictive aspect of smoking, it is possible for people to stop if their motivation is strong enough and they receive proper support, and stopping produces almost immediate benefits to health.

Although the risks to the smoker have been understood for some time, the most recent work suggests that smoking is also bad for the health of non-smokers who are exposed to it. Concern over the dangers of 'passive smoking' has led to increasing calls for the protection of non-smokers and the introduction of effective workplace smoking policies. Such policies are best developed through consultation and need to be fair to smokers as well as non-smokers.

Why smoking at work is an issue for managers

Smoking at work raises two key issues: first, looking at the worker who smokes, there is overwhelming evidence of the potential smoking has to damage that person's health and probably shorten his or her life; second, non-smokers who are exposed to tobacco smoke at work often find the environment uncomfortable – which affects morale and productivity – and there is increasing evidence of harm to non-smokers from 'passive smoking'.

These issues cannot be ignored by employers. If people smoking at work is a hazard to other people's health, then it is logical that action should be taken, just as action would be taken to control, say, a hazard to health arising from a chemical used in the manufacturing process.

The Royal College of Physicians has estimated that smoking-induced illness accounts for at least 50 million lost working days a year. According to Department of Health figures, this equates to a likely cost in terms of lost production of between £2200 and £3200 million. The argument that smoking is a private issue which concerns no one but the smoker is increasingly losing ground as organisations conclude that they must do something to address such a significant cause of ill-health and lost time.

The risk to the smoker

'A custom loathsome to the eye, harmful to the brain, dangerous to the lungs, and in the black stinking fume thereof, nearest resembling the horrible Stygian smoke of the pit that is bottomless.'
James I of England (1604)

The potential of smoking to damage the smoker's health is well-documented. Writing in the Health Education Journal in 1980, Richard Peto gave a useful yardstick of risk with his estimate that, of 1000 young UK smokers of 20 or more cigarettes a day, one will be murdered, six will die in road accidents and 250 will die prematurely as a result of their smoking. The most up-to-date estimate is that each year in the UK, 110,000 people are killed by smoking.

Lung cancer

The increased risk of lung cancer is the first thing many people think of, but it is worth highlighting just how significant this is. In 1912, there were 374 cases of lung cancer world-wide, and the disease occurred so rarely that it was thought to be hereditary. In the USA it is now estimated that there are between 120,000 and 140,000 lung cancer deaths per year and that just under 400,000 Americans die annually from the effects of smoking.

In Britain we have the highest lung cancer rate in the world with about 40,000 people a year dying from this cause. There is little doubt that this is directly linked to cigarette smoking, with the risk of developing lung cancer strongly related to the number of cigarettes smoked.

Although lung cancer is the main problem – nine out of ten lung cancer deaths are attributable to smoking – smokers are also at risk from other cancers including those of the mouth, nose and throat. There is also a strong association between smoking and cancers of the bladder, kidney, pancreas, stomach and – in women – the uterus. Mothers who smoke during pregnancy are more likely to miscarry or have the child stillborn, and the child's birth weight is on average lower than that of children born to non-smoking mothers.

The potential harm of cigarette smoking may well be increased when combined with exposure to other factors. The most famous example of this is documented in a study of just under 18,000 asbestos workers over ten years. The results showed that the relative risk of dying from lung cancer was 5 for asbestos workers who did not smoke and 11 for smokers who were not exposed to asbestos. However, for smokers who were also exposed to asbestos, the relative risk rose to 53.

Heart disease

In addition to these findings, there is conclusive evidence that cigarette smoking is one of the most important risk factors for the biggest single cause of premature death in the UK – coronary heart disease (CHD). Diseases of the heart and arteries are a major cause of premature death in most industrial countries. In the UK, more people died during the 1980s from CHD than from all forms of cancer combined and CHD alone accounted for 30 per cent of deaths in men and 25 per cent of deaths in women.

Smoking is not the only risk factor for CHD, but it is a major one, with a direct link between the length of time for which the individual has smoked and the risk of developing cardiovascular disease. In comparison with a non-smoker, a person who smokes cigarettes is about twice as likely to have a heart attack, and also runs an increased risk of having a stroke.

The link between smoking and increased risk of CHD has not been fully explained, although it has been suggested that:

- smoking increases the release of noradrenaline, which in turn increases the heart's workload;
- smoking induces chemical agents which enhance atherosclerosis (hardening of the arteries);
- smoking increases blood pressure – in itself a major risk factor for CHD;
- cigarette smoke contains carbon monoxide, which bonds more strongly than oxygen with the red blood cells, thus effectively reducing the oxygen carrying capacity of the blood. This in turn aggravates the effect of any other condition – such as narrowing of the arteries – which starves the heart muscle of oxygen. This is a double problem, because the heart has to work harder to supply

the same amount of oxygen to the rest of the body. Being a muscle itself, it too needs oxygen, and hence has to meet the extra demand with a reduced amount of oxygen available from the bloodstream.

It is also worth noting that, where people succeed in giving up smoking, a prompt decline in risk of CHD is seen.

So great is the damage to health associated with smoking that reducing tobacco use/consumption is the top strategic objective of public health programmes in both the US and the UK. At the workplace level it has frequently been suggested that the single most effective thing an employer can do to maintain and improve the health of the workforce is to encourage people to give up smoking. It has also been suggested that the cheapest and most effective form of health screening for CHD, lung cancer and chronic bronchitis is the simple question 'do you smoke?'

The risk to the non-smoker

Passive smoking

The danger of passive or involuntary smoking – breathing in other people's tobacco smoke – has received great attention, and is now an issue that cannot be ignored in the hope that it will go away. If smoking is only dangerous to the smoker, then it could be said that this is the individual's own concern and nobody else's. But if smoking puts others at risk as well, then clearly issues other than the individual smoker's freedom come into play.

This view was summed up by John Hougham, Ford's Personnel Director, quoted in *The Times*:

'Our policy makes it clear that it is not a ban on smoking. Ford does not set itself up as a guardian. We respect an employee's right to decide whether to smoke, but it was thought that to allow non-smokers to continue to be exposed to proven health risks was inconsistent with Ford's role as a responsible employer. We intend to reduce employees' exposure to passive smoking.'

If cigarette smoke is bad for the smoker, there is really no logical reason why it should not also be bad for the non-smoker. Indeed, given that cigarette smoke contains not only carbon monoxide but also such recognised carcinogens (cancer causing chemicals) as dimethylnitrosamine, hydrazine, vinyl chloride and benzo(A)pyrene, it would

---

be surprising if it did not cause ill-health effects in non-smokers as well as smokers.

The evidence for the dangers of passive smoking is now impossible to ignore. In 1986 the US Surgeon General's Report found that non-smokers exposed to tobacco smoke in the environment suffer from more respiratory illness and eye irritation than do those not so exposed, and went on to conclude that involuntary smoking is a cause of disease, including lung cancer, in non-smokers.

In 1987, history was made when an Australian bus driver, Sean Carroll, won a significant out of court settlement after medical evidence presented to a tribunal suggested that he had contracted lung cancer as a result of his working environment – an often packed single decker bus, with no smoking restrictions and no partition to protect the driver. He himself had never smoked, nor had any member of his family.

A year later the UK Independent Scientific Committee on Smoking and Health concluded that 'passive smoking is associated with an increased risk of lung cancer in non-smokers' and it is now thought that several hundred of the 40,000 or so deaths from lung cancer each year in the UK could be due to passive smoking. If this is true it could mean that as many people die each year as a result of passive smoking as are killed in industrial accidents in the whole of the manufacturing and construction industries.

Similar figures are contained in *Passive Smoking: a Health Hazard*, a report published in 1991. This was prepared by the Imperial Cancer Research Fund and the Cancer Research Campaign and supported by more than 30 organisations including the Royal College of Physicians, the British Medical Association, and the British Lung Foundation. Dr Spencer Haggard, the Chief Executive of the Health Education Authority, states the position:

'There is a clear scientific case for taking action to restrict smoking in public places. We expect members of parliament to press for legislation to protect non-smokers, and employers to introduce, implement and monitor strict smoking control policies at every workplace in the country. They owe their employees nothing less.'

Although legal action such as that taken by Sean Carroll is rare, there is no doubt that the diminishing number of smokers, coupled with concern about hazards to health (both that of the smoker and that of his/her colleagues) is putting employers under increasing pressure to devise and implement smoking policies. In the remainder of this chapter, we look at the issues involved in setting up a smoking policy in the workplace and explore ways of helping smokers who want to give up to do so successfully.

Setting up a smoking policy

Rationale

There are a number of powerful arguments for setting up an effective smoking policy. Most studies show that smokers are now in the minority, making up only around 20 per cent of the working population. With greater awareness of the dangers of passive smoking, non-smokers are increasingly asserting their desire (many would say their right) to work in a smoke-free environment.

We have seen in the last few years a massive upsurge of interest in all aspects of the environment, and this naturally includes for most people the environment within the office or the factory where they work. This in turn is likely to increase the pressure on employers to do something about cigarette smoke in the workplace.

In 1988, a government report recommended that, in view of increasing evidence about the dangers of passive smoking, non-smoking should be considered the norm in enclosed workplace areas. At the same time, many organisations are studying or implementing more broadly-based employee wellness programmes. As cigarette smoking is such an important risk factor, not only for cancer, but also for cardiovascular disease and for respiratory problems such as bronchitis and emphysema, many managers are now seeing action to discourage people from smoking at work as a priority.

Apart from the hazards to health, smoking significantly increases the risk of fire in a workplace – smoking materials, electrical faults and malicious ignition being the three most important causes of fires in industrial and commercial premises. It is important that there is a proper policy and not just a statement of good intent, or indeed a free-for-all in which the onus is placed on individual working groups (e.g. those who share an office) to come up with their own solution. People do need to know where they stand, and what their employer's stance is.

The smokers' reaction

Having identified the need to take action, some organisations have hesitated do to so, fearing that they will antagonise smokers. However, this is not necessarily the case. A 1986 MORI poll found that less than 25 per cent of smokers were in favour of smoking being allowed in all areas of the workplace. Interestingly, 85 per cent of non-smokers believed that smoking should either be allowed only in specific designated areas, or not permitted at all.

Although there are exceptions, our experience is that smokers are increasingly concerned about the effect of their smoking on their colleagues, and in this context it is interesting that an NOP poll for the London Evening Standard in 1987 found that 81 per cent of smokers agreed with the statement 'in general, people who do not smoke should have the right to work in air free from tobacco smoke.'

As the charity Action on Smoking and Health (ASH) points out, work is now one of the few places where people have no choice about whether to breathe air that contains cigarette smoke.

Consult, then act

Consultation is crucial to the successful implementation of a smoking policy. Suddenly imposing unilateral restrictions without adequate discussion and reasonable lead time will certainly cause friction. It could even be viewed as a breach of contract. Adequate consultation should avoid the possibility of smokers resigning and then claiming compensation for constructive dismissal.

Much has been written about implementing smoking policies, including the Health Education Authority book *Smoking Policies at Work* and ASH's own *Smoking policy manual*. However, the five key steps can be summed up as follows:

- set up a working party, which should be representative of the workforce and include smokers and non-smokers;
- define the issue, which is about smoking and not about smokers. Information about hazards should be circulated and discussion encouraged;
- consult the workforce and make sure they are all aware of what is being done;
- draw up the policy, making it clear how it will be enforced;
- implement the policy. This starts with communicating it to the workforce. A clear implementation date should be set. This should allow a reasonable time for adjustment, but the delay should not be so great that the project loses impetus.

Avoiding pitfalls

The essential thing to remember is that there is nothing radically different between implementing a smoking policy and managing any other sort of change. While it is true that smoking can become a polarised issue, with feelings running very strongly on both sides, this is equally true of many other issues which managers face every day. What follows from this is that the key points for success in managing sensitive issues generally are also the key points for the successful implementation of a smoking policy. These can be summarised as follows:

1. THERE NEEDS TO BE A PLAN

The introduction of a smoking policy should not be done on a flying by the seat of the pants basis. There needs to be a clear plan, including a rationale (why we are doing this), an agreed timescale and clear allocation of responsibilities.

2. THE APPROACH SHOULD BE POSITIVE

People generally respond better to the carrot than to the stick, and the introduction of a smoking policy is more likely to be smooth if it is presented in terms of the benefits it will produce, e.g. better motivated staff working in a better environment, less friction between smokers and non-smokers, reduced risk of fire, more agreeable surroundings for customers and visitors.

3. LEAD FROM THE TOP

In most organisations, projects of whatever sort are far more likely to be successful if they have the backing and support of senior managers. This in turn implies that the case for a smoking policy needs to be properly presented, with the appropriate supporting information, to senior managers.

4. TALK TO PEOPLE

As indicated above, a smoking policy is unlikely to succeed without effective consultation. Most managers find that people are best motivated by a sense of involvement and a perception that they have some say in decisions that affect their working environment. There are several different ways of doing this. Large organisations often have a consultative framework already in place for other purposes. A questionnaire is a simple and reasonably quick way of getting people's views. One company simply put up a large whiteboard on a stand in its offices, together with some pens, and invited employees to note their feelings. While this approach could be criticised on some grounds, at least it gave managers a better insight into employees' views.

5. DELIVER THE GOODS

Written policies are an essential feature of business life, but we must remember that people tend to judge by what they see happening in practice rather than by the words on paper. So, if the policy promises practical help for people who want to give up smoking, this must be made available. Equally, if the policy says that after a particular date, smoking in designated 'no smoking' areas will be treated as a disciplinary matter, then this must be enforced, otherwise the whole credibility of the policy – and indeed, of the management – will be undermined.

6. MONITOR

Each stage of implementation should have a built-in monitoring element, so that any necessary adjustments can be made. Without this, key aspects may be forgotten and if no action is taken, problems could arise. For example, what is being done to make visitors aware of the policy – do they know where they can and cannot smoke? What about recruitment and induction? Is it made clear in job advertisements and the recruitment process as a whole that a smoking policy is in force? Are the arrangements explained to new starters as part of induction training?

7. FOLLOW-UP

Once the policy is operating, it is a good idea to follow-up at some reasonable time interval, to see that all is operating as intended and that any difficulties have been ironed out, but above all to find out if the policy overall has achieved what was intended.

ASH has suggested a practical checklist for assessing policies on smoking – see Figure 8.1.

- does it protect the non-smoker?
- does it meet the working party's objectives?
- can it be implemented consistently?
- will it be seen as fair by all employees?
- will it be relatively easy to administer?
- does it name the person responsible for monitoring and receiving feedback?
- does it show how disagreements are to be resolved?
- does it show how breaches will be dealt with?
- does it make clear what help and support there will be for smokers?

Figure 8.1 ASH checklist for smoking policies

Support for the smoker

When introducing a smoking policy, it is vital that the smoking is not confused with smokers – that is to say, it is the behaviour rather than the individual person that is undesirable. We may condemn smoking as a habit which is bad for the health of the smoker and also (in the light of the latest evidence) hazardous to others as well. But it is important not to fall into the trap of taking a moralistic or condemnatory attitude towards individuals.

The approach taken will vary, depending on the nature of the smoking policy introduced. For example, where a partial ban is introduced, there will by definition still be areas in which people are permitted to smoke. Where all smoking in the workplace is discouraged or banned, then support must be given to help people who wish to stop smoking to do so. Given the evidence of damage to the smoker's own health, many organisations will decide that such support is an essential feature of the overall healthcare programme in any case.

Many smokers would like to give up. Smokers often say this, and a survey conducted in the USA in 1985–6 showed that 70 per cent of the adults surveyed had made at least one serious attempt to give up smoking, and one third had stopped for at least one day during the year of questioning. The introduction of a policy which restricts smoking at work may well be a turning point in helping smokers achieve something which they wish to do, and perhaps have wanted to do for a long time.

Giving up is hard

The evidence of the damage smoking does to the smoker's health is overwhelming. Indeed, so great is the number of studies which have focused on the health risks of smoking that Fletcher Knebel wrote, as long ago as 1961, tongue in cheek:

'It is now proved beyond doubt that smoking is one of the leading causes of statistics.'

While at a rational level, the evidence cannot be ignored, many people still continue to smoke, and there is some evidence that the reduction in the number of people who smoke may be levelling off or even going into reverse.

Stopping, then, is clearly not just a matter of an intellectual decision, based on the evidence of damage to health (although for many people, this is the biggest factor in their decision to stop). One of the most significant points is that smoking – and especially nicotine – is addictive.

MINERVA
HEALTH MANAGEMENT

MINERVA ADVICE SHEET

Stopping Smoking

Smoking is the single, most preventable, cause of disease. Heart disease, lung cancer, bronchitis and a host of other problems arise from cigarette smoking. Everyone knows that they should stop but for many the hurdle just seems too large. However, it is possible if approached the right way.

Smoking is a habit. Breaking it is not easy and the effort required should not be underestimated.

First Steps

1. **Set a date** on which you will stop - think of a good day, potentially free from stress about ten to fourteen days ahead.

2. **Tell people**, and get them to help and encourage you - especially your partner. Try to get them to join you.

3. **Think** about your smoking - where do you smoke? Keep notes on places and times when you take a cigarette, so you can avoid these situations later.

4. **Plan** other activities as a reward for not smoking. Buy some new clothes, take up a new sport (use your cigarette money to buy new equipment - golf clubs, squash racquet, etc.).

Figure 8.2   Advice sheet – stopping smoking

Indeed, in 1988 the US Surgeon General concluded not only that cigarettes (and other forms of tobacco) are addictive, and that nicotine is the main component causing the addiction, but also that the addiction derived from tobacco is similar to that for drugs such as cocaine and heroin.

But there is also evidence that the addiction is behavioural as well as physiological. This is borne out by those who only smoke at certain times of the day, or in certain places. Many smokers say that the cigarette smoked with coffee after dinner is the hardest one to give up! Smoking may also be one of the mechanisms by which people cope with stress. The conclusion from this is that to help people stop

The Big Day

The night before throw away all cigarettes, matches, lighters and ashtrays.

On the morning, eat a good breakfast with a different menu from normal. Fill your time until you start work with an activity that distracts you from thinking about smoking.

Avoid situations and group activities where you always smoke. Go out for a walk, or shop, rather than kill time during your lunch break.

Take each day, one at a time. Mark a calendar as you progress through your first week and first month.

<u>Don't</u> try to taper off - STOP COMPLETELY.

<u>Don't</u> substitute pipes or cigars.

<u>Don't</u> worry about gaining weight. Two thirds of all people who stop smoking do **not** put on weight. Those who do tend to lose it after a short while as the body readjusts to its new environment.

REMEMBER

Smoking cigarettes releases powerful chemicals into your body - do not expect their withdrawal after years to be simple. Often special nicotine chewing gum can help in the early days - ask your doctor about this.

FINALLY

1. Eat well -
   especially fresh fruit, raw vegetables, raisins, nuts and fruit juices.

2. Drink plenty of water.

GOOD LUCK !

smoking, you have to understand why they smoke, and clearly, simply quoting the research findings about the damage to health is not that helpful by itself.

Many techniques have been used to help smokers give up. These include:

- counselling;
- group therapy;
- medication;
- use of nicotine chewing gum;
- phased reduction coupled with support;
- demonstration of carbon monoxide in exhaled breath;

- acupuncture;
- hypnotism;
- shock therapy.

People differ in how, what, when, where and why they smoke – and also in what they find is the greatest obstacle to stopping. That said, and taking into account the point made above about the physiological and psychological factors, it is unlikely that there is a single 'best' technique for helping people to stop smoking. The most effective programmes are likely to use a combination of methods – the so-called 'multicomponent' or 'broad spectrum' approach.

Whatever method is used, it helps to give smokers practical guidelines which they can take away and use to structure their own approach to stopping smoking. These might be in the form of a booklet such as 'So you want to stop smoking' (Health Education Authority) or a simple advice sheet such as that shown in Figure 8.2.

As with any other aspect of corporate healthcare, proper planning, a consistent approach and a firm commitment are needed if the 'stop smoking' programme is going to succeed. However, organisations who do run effective programmes can take comfort from the fact that there is almost no other initiative they could take which would do more to improve their employees' health and the quality of the working environment.

CHECKLIST

- Do we know what our employees think about smoking and what proportion of them smokes?
- Is there currently a policy on smoking at work?
- If not, what would be the most effective way of introducing a smoking policy? – and in particular:
- What would be the best way to consult our employees?
- What sort of restriction on smoking would be most fair and what is the most effective means of communicating the policy to employees?
- Is there a proper lead-in time to allow people to get used to the new arrangements?
- Is the policy supported by senior managers?
- How strong a line will be taken with anyone not complying with the proposed arrangements?
- What support will be given to smokers who want to give up smoking?
- Where does smoking fit within our overall policy on employee health and welfare?

CHAPTER 9
Fitness and Exercise

Exercise makes a positive contribution to many aspects of health, promotes a feeling of well being and helps to reduce stress. However, the benefits of exercise cannot be stored, and can only be achieved with a permanent adjustment to lifestyle. Many options exist for those wishing to improve their fitness, ranging from group exercises and competitive sport, to solitary fitness programmes.

Employers can benefit in a number of ways from encouraging fitness in employees. Fit people work better, are more content, and have less absenteeism than others. Employers can take many initiatives to encourage fitness, including the provision of exercise facilities at work, and the sponsorship of employee sporting activities.

Employers can also introduce fitness testing, sometimes in association with other health screening services. Such testing takes a number of forms, but promotes interest in fitness and enables exercise programmes to be specifically designed for the individual. All support for employee fitness at work demonstrates the commitment of the employer to the mental and physical health of the workforce.

Fitness is fashionable. In fact a browse through the average sports shop with its designer running shoes and carbon fibre racquets, might suggest that fitness *is* fashion. This book has already noted that there is a difference between fitness and health, but is there also a connection? Are fit people healthy? Do they live longer? Do they work better? This chapter considers these questions, and looks at practical measures which will benefit both employers and employees.

The benefits of exercise

There have been several studies which have looked for a connection between physical activity and health. One of the first and still best known, was undertaken in the early 1950s amongst employees of London Transport. This showed that bus conductors had significantly less heart disease than bus drivers. The conclusion was that the higher activity levels involved in the conductors' work were giving them protection which was not provided by the more sedentary work of the drivers. In fact, this study was criticised because it was found that different types of people took up the two different jobs. Therefore the difference in heart disease could have been caused by differences in the people rather than their work. Nevertheless, the study created much interest, and opened the way for further studies – some of which are still continuing.

In one recent report published by the British Heart Foundation, 'Exercise and the Heart', it was said that physical inactivity in men represents an increased risk of heart disease in line with that of high blood pressure, raised cholesterol, or smoking about 20 cigarettes per day. Studies of desk-bound senior executives found that those who took part in vigorous physical activity had, over an eight year period, less than half the incidence of coronary heart disease than their more sedentary colleagues.

It is possible to itemise a number of direct, measurable effects which result from exercise:

- cardiovascular function is improved;
- work effort can be more sustained;
- muscle strength is increased;
- blood pressure is reduced;
- the risk of obesity is reduced;
- the risk of osteoporosis (bone thinning) is reduced;
- total blood cholesterol level is reduced, and HDL cholesterol (which offers protection) is increased.

It would be expected that changes like these should make a real contribution to personal health, and be reflected in an extended lifespan for those who exercise. This is indeed being borne out by research studies. A follow up of Harvard University graduates showed that people who are physically active live up to 2.5 years longer than those who are relatively inactive. The benefits of exercise seem to be obtained when a total of at least one hour's vigorous activity is undertaken each week. Vigorous exercise is that which requires an energy expenditure of 7.7 kilocalories per minute, and includes swimming, cycling and jogging. The general consensus of exercise specialists is that a good exercise pattern is 20 to 30 minutes three times per week. It is worth noting some other findings of the research to date:

- the benefits of exercise cannot be 'stored' for long. The benefits of an exercise session decay exponentially over ten days. Athletes who have become sedentary fall into the same risk group as those who have always been sedentary;
- the corollary of the above is more cheering – it is that previous lack of exercise is no barrier to becoming fit. The benefits of exercise can be produced over a three month period. Of course the exercise must then be continued if the benefit is to be maintained;
- the benefits of exercise exist at all age ranges. Provided exercise is started safely (see later), there is no age barrier;
- exercise appears to be an *independent* factor in protecting against heart disease. In other words, it does not produce benefit merely because of its effect of reducing blood pressure, weight, etc.

Exercise after a heart attack

In the 1930s and 40s, when coronary heart disease was relatively rare, the surviving victim of a heart attack was required to avoid all physical exertion for a period of several months. It has now become clear that a programme of medically supervised exercise can convey positive benefits to the post-heart attack victim, and aid both physical and mental recovery. The strengthening effect of exercise reduces the work load demanded of the heart and increases tolerance of effort. People can cope more easily with the demands of everyday life, and can deal more safely with the occasional demands for vigorous effort which inevitably occur.

Effects on mental health

An extremely common reaction to exercise is a feeling of well-being, associated with enhanced self-confidence, pride, and a feeling of being in control. Doctors have discovered that some patients with symptoms of depression, including some who have not responded to drug treatment, can be cured with exercise alone. To some extent this effect can be explained by the biochemical effects of substances such as the endorphins and enkephalins which are produced in the brain during physical exertion. These are natural morphine-type substances which suppress pain and induce a feeling of euphoria. They account for the 'high' of the long distance runner, and it seems likely that for some people, sustained exercise is literally addictive. However, to dismiss the psychological benefits of exercise as entirely drug-induced would be inaccurate – since drugs alone do not produce the same effects. There is a growing body of opinion that the explanation is based on the inter-relationship between mind and body, and that understanding this type of effect will be the key to future developments in healthcare.

Benefits to employers

Many of the benefits of a fitter workforce are self-evident. Fitter people can do their job better and, as noted above, their fitness will contribute to their overall health. In consequence, many employers are totally committed to promoting health at work. This is especially the case in the Far East, and everyone will have seen film of employees in Japanese companies joining in mass exercise programmes. The managers of these companies are not motivated entirely by altruism – they know that exercise is good for business. Exercise benefits employers in a number of ways:

1. REDUCED ABSENTEEISM

It is generally accepted that a high absence rate is linked with lack of fitness, and a number of studies seem to confirm this observation – though more work is still needed. Research in this area is difficult, because of the problem of finding groups of people who are similar in every respect other than their exercise level. However, the fact is that the organisations which actively promote and encourage the fitness of their employees are those with the lowest absence rates.

2. SATISFACTION WITH THE EMPLOYER

Good employees can afford to pick and choose their employers. Attractive employers are those who show a commitment to their employees – and a commitment to fitness in the sorts of ways which will be considered later, is a sign not just of caring but of *vitality*. Exercise programmes, sports sponsorship, etc, show a vigour which is appreciated by the type of people most organisations wish to employ.

3. REDUCED STRESS

As discussed, exercise has a positive effect on mental well-being, an important requirement if employees are to give of their best. It is often said that stress builds up in modern life because we are denied the 'fight or flight' response. In other words, stress causes harm because we can no longer make the physical response to it which is our natural, evolved reaction. Exercise is the ideal compromise when stress builds up at work – where fleeing is impossible, and fighting is frowned on!

What about the risks?

The risks of exercise are highly publicised because they can be dramatic – the sudden death of someone who seemed perfectly well until they played squash. There is no doubt that the extremely small risk of sudden death (which is almost always due to pre-existing heart disease) is outweighed by the longer term benefits of improved health. But no risk should be tolerated if it can be avoided, and no-one should suddenly embark on vigorous exercise after a long period of inactivity. Exercise should be built up gradually starting with gentle exercise for 10 minutes daily, increasing over 6–8 weeks to 20 or 30 minutes of vigorous exercise every other day. Those who are overweight, hypertensive, over 50, or unsure about their health should definitely consult their GP first.

This suggests a clear benefit for the employer being involved in fitness programmes. Exercise can be introduced in an informed way, graded programmes can be provided by the employer, and regular monitoring of progress can be arranged. The employer can also arrange to provide information and facilities to safeguard against the injury risks of some sports. These include eye injuries from ball games, and sprains and fractures from activities such as running. Again, these risks are outweighed by the benefits, but still justify careful planning to avoid. Good coaching, proper choice of clothing, and the right equipment, are all elements of safe exercise – and can all be covered in programmes organised by the responsible employer. In considering safety precautions to be coupled with the introduction of exercise, it is worth noting that far and away the most dangerous sport, when measured by annual death rate, is swimming. About 200 people are drowned each year in Great Britain – the majority through unorganised swimming in lakes and the sea. By contrast, swimming comes near the bottom of the *injury* ranking with only about three injuries for every thousand participants each year. At the top of the injury list come skiing and rugby, each with about 50 injuries per thousand participants each year.

What is fitness?

Fitness is a somewhat elusive quality – though you know when you've got it. Fitness is not a scientific term, and has no strict definition, but is essentially having the capacity to cope with physical demands on the body. It is generally considered in three categories – strength, suppleness, and stamina.

Strength is the ability to exert force in pulling, pushing and lifting.

Strength is a continual everyday requirement, and we regularly encounter the limits of our strength – in picking up loads, driving in screws, etc. A high level of strength is protection against sprains and strains, and improves posture. Strength is developed by exercising muscles against resistance.

Suppleness is the ability to stretch, twist and bend the neck, trunk and limbs through a range of movements. Suppleness also gives protection against injury, and is another everyday requirement – for getting in and out of cars and baths, playing with children, doing awkward jobs, etc. Suppleness is improved by exercises that stretch the muscles that work the joints.

Stamina is the ability to keep going without becoming tired quickly. Stamina enables you to keep up with other active people, and to press on with tiring jobs. Activities which improve stamina are those which are energetic and sustained. They are also the activities that give protection against heart disease.

Measuring fitness

As discussed in Chapter 3, testing of employees for fitness is an extremely popular form of health screening – it appeals to people who take a particular interest in their health. It is a valuable component of many corporate healthcare programmes and can be used both to devise suitable exercise programmes – especially for those who have not exercised for some time – and to monitor progress towards personal fitness targets.

Before discussing sophisticated testing, there are some rule-of-thumb approaches which can be used to gauge fitness. The average middle-aged man or woman, not particularly involved in regular sport, should be able to:

- comfortably walk ten miles at normal walking pace;
- comfortably walk one mile at a brisk pace;
- run up a flight of 20 steps without distress;
- run 30 metres in less than seven seconds.

As with *all* physical activity, a doctor should be consulted if there is discomfort, or if activity is being started after a long period without exercise.

A simple test to measure fitness is based on checking pulse rate after a period of controlled exercise. This requires finding a convenient step which is 200 mm (8 inches) high. For three minutes step up and down at the rate of two movements every five seconds – a movement is one foot up, the other foot up, one foot down, the other foot down. After the three minutes, sit and rest for one minute. Then check pulse rate – the following guide will indicate the level of fitness.

Pulse rate (beats per minute)		
Men	Women	Fitness level
<80	<85	very fit
80–89	85–94	fit
90–100	95–110	unfit
>100	>110	very unfit

Clinical measurements

In the controlled environment of a clinic – or a workplace provided with suitable equipment, a range of scientific tests can be undertaken which give more precise information about fitness. As discussed in Chapter 3, such tests often incorporate computer analysis to interpret the results, and provide graded programmes for sports or exercises chosen by the individual. Since 'fitness' is not a specific, scientific measurement, a number of evaluations might be included in fitness screening.

Heart rate will be measured at rest and during controlled exercise using an exercise ergometer – a static cycle or treadmill which can be precisely adjusted to a specified energy output. Heart rate can be measured simply by taking the pulse, but might also be monitored electronically. As shown by the above rule of thumb test, as fitness improves, the same work load will be achieved at lower heart rates.

Body fat will be measured or estimated. This might be based on height and weight measurements from which the 'Body Mass Index' is calculated. The Body Mass Index is the individual's weight in kilograms divided by the square of their height in metres. An acceptable Body Mass Index is around 20 to 25 in men, and 19 to 24 in women, with levels above about 30 counting as obesity. Body fat can also be measured using specially calibrated callipers which measure the thickness of a pinch of flesh, usually at the back of the upper arm, above the shoulder blade, and at the top of the hip bone and abdomen.

These measurements can be used to produce a direct calculation of body fat, with levels under about 15 per cent being good, and levels over about 30 per cent being badly overweight. It is also possible to measure body fat using electronic devices which directly gauge the depth of the fat layer.

Lung function can be expected to improve with exercise, so might also be measured within a fitness test. Lung function testing, or spirometry, involves blowing as hard as possible down a tube into an instrument which measures the volume of air and the rate at which it is exhaled. The usual measurements are the FEV1, or Forced Expired Volume – the amount of air which can be forced out of the lungs in the standard time of one second, the FVC, or Forced Vital Capacity – the amount of air that can be taken in one breath, and the TLC, or total lung capacity. The results are then compared with 'expected' results for someone of that age, height and sex, and expressed as a percentage of predicted value. It is also possible that a Gas Transfer Test will be undertaken. This measures the efficiency of the lungs at transferring oxygen into the blood, and removing carbon dioxide from it. The test involves breathing into and out of a bag which is connected to a gas analyser.

Blood pressure will be monitored – possibly on a regular basis during exercise, electrocardiography or ECG may be undertaken to spot any irregularities of the heart rhythm, while strength can be measured by observing the power of the muscles against known weights or tension. A common test uses the grip dynamometer which shows the strength of the hand's grip on a calibrated dial. Suppleness may be observed by seeing how flexible the body is against graduated scales. For example, how far from the feet the floor can be touched (if at all!), and how far forward the hands can be pushed when sitting with legs outstretched.

Types of exercise

Advising employees on suitable exercise programmes is not unlike giving career advice. Someone in the organisation has to undertake to match the interests and abilities of each employee, with the range of options available. There are probably at least 50 exercises or sports widely practised in Great Britain. This section reviews some of the most popular, and provides information which would be relevant to the average employee.

Before proceeding it is essential to repeat that no-one should embark on exercise after a long period of inactivity without following certain basic precautions. The do's and don'ts are:

- do consult a doctor if you have not exercised for a long time, or if you have conditions such as heart disease, diabetes, high blood pressure, chest trouble, joint pains, dizziness, or back pain;

- do start gently, and gradually build up the exercise level;
- do stop and rest immediately if you feel discomfort;
- do exercise regularly – ideally two or three times a week;
- don't exercise straight after a heavy meal;
- don't deliberately exercise until you feel pain;
- don't exercise if you have a heavy cold or feel unwell.

Before looking at specific exercises, we should consider some terminology. This has tended to become rather complicated as exercise has become big business. Exercise falls into two main categories – aerobic and anaerobic. Aerobic exercise is designed to increase the intake of oxygen, and includes the vigorous exercises that increase the rate of the heart and lungs. Swimming and jogging are examples of aerobic exercises. So too is organised 'aerobic' exercising – usually with an encouraging leader, and exhilarating music. Aerobic exercise is the type of exercise needed to strengthen the heart, and reduce the risk of coronary heart disease. Anaerobic exercise, on the other hand, is designed to directly strengthen particular groups of muscles, and includes weight lifting and circuit training. Other terms used for exercise tend to be 'brand-names' for particular exercise programmes or techniques. These include the 'Y-Plan' aerobic exercise programme, 'Isometrics' – which involve muscular effort against immovable objects such as walls, and 'Callanetics' – a programme of exercises to increase suppleness and strength without any physical impact, developed by Callan Pinckney.

We will now consider a handful of the most popular exercises at the present time, and see how they match the requirements of an employee considering the challenge of becoming fit. It would be unrealistic to review all 50 of the exercises in regular practice, but these should at least give a picture against which others can be compared.

Badminton

An excellent sport with widely accessible facilities. The slowness of the shuttle makes it suitable for all ages and all levels of fitness. Good for cardiovascular fitness, strength (especially of the legs), and stamina. Costs of equipment and clothing are reasonable. Perhaps one of the ideal games for company competitions because of its suitability for a wide range of individuals at all times of the year.

Bowling

A sociable game, excellent for company competitions, though its image is of a game for the elderly rather than the young. Not an aerobic sport, it improves flexibility in the shoulders and arms, and strength in the legs. Bowling can be played indoors or outside, with facilities in many towns and villages.

Cycling

An ideal activity for overall fitness, building up stamina and leg strength. Less effective for developing suppleness, but particularly good for those with leg or back problems. Not so accessible as a competitive sport – needs to be taken seriously. Some risk of accidents on busy roads, and knowledge of highway safety is essential. The risks can be avoided with a static exercise bike at home – though for many people the improved safety is outweighed by the boredom!

Dance

Increasingly popular, and introduces music and an opportunity to be creative. Highly sociable, it provides excellent exercise for strength, particularly of the legs, stamina, and suppleness. There are many facilities for dancing, including education classes, throughout the country. Options are available to suit all tastes and age ranges.

Exercise

Exercise classes and facilities are widely available, and on the increase. Exercise programmes include aerobics, and classes for various age ranges. Exercises are available for improving strength, stamina, and suppleness. For beginners, much depends on the knowledge and enthusiasm of the teacher. For sufficiently large organisations, exercise facilities are a first-class benefit.

Golf

More energetic than non-golfers realise, though aerobic exercise is not sustained. Good for stamina and leg strength if played regularly. Often an expensive sport, unless the local authority provides facilities. Otherwise equipment and club membership can be costly. Company competitions are often organised and can be taken extremely seriously. For many people the main drawback is that golf is a time consuming way of keeping fit.

Jogging and running

Now enormously popular as a way of keeping fit. Very convenient and inexpensive, it can be solitary or sociable, with jogging and running groups everywhere. Often supported by employers, many companies encouraging lunch-time runs etc. Aerobic exercise, and a quick way to get fit. Good for stamina, not so good for suppleness or upper body strength. Some injury risk, especially to knees and ankles. Essential to wear good running shoes, and to start gently.

Martial arts and judo

Practised throughout Britain, following origination in the Far East. Examples are karate, aikido, and jiu jitsu. Limited value as cardiovascular exercise, but good for muscle strength and suppleness. Their popularity is partly because of their value in self-defence, and some self-defence training uses a combination of martial arts skills. Some risk of physical injury, so good instruction is essential.

Snooker

Only just counts as exercise! Good for relaxation. Definitely not aerobic, but appealing to a wide range of people, and capable of development to a very high skill level. Popular in companies with the space for a table, though best if provided alongside more energetic activities.

Squash

An extremely demanding game, providing stamina, suppleness and leg strength. Not a game to take up to get fit – get fit first! Facilities widely available at low cost. Squash has a reputation as a dangerous game, mainly resulting from incidents when competitive middle-aged men have played after a period of inactivity.

Swimming

Perhaps *the* ideal exercise. One of the most widely available sports, improving cardiovascular fitness, and building strength, stamina and suppleness. Especially good for those who are overweight, or who have backache or disability, because of the support given by the water. The best exercise is 'lane' swimming, but swimming can also be a social activity. Surveys amongst employee groups show swimming to be the sport most people would like to take up – and would therefore strongly justify support and sponsorship from employers. Facilities are expensive to build and maintain, but many employers have negotiated group discounts with local public and private facilities.

Tennis

A popular sport, though hard to play throughout the year due to lack of indoor facilities. Exercise value increases as skill improves, when it becomes good for stamina, suppleness and leg strength. Can be played by most ages, though harder to pick up than badminton or squash.

Team games

There are too many team games to review separately. The most popular include basketball, cricket, football, hockey, rounders and rugby. Most team games are good for stamina and strength, and reasonably good for suppleness. They also have some of the highest injury risks, so proper clothing is important. Team games are ideal for companies and there are many opportunities for competing with other organisations. As well as fitness there are benefits from team building, and development of pride in the organisation.

Walking

Brisk walking is excellent for stamina, but not for suppleness or strength – ideal if combined with other forms of exercise. Walking is a highly organised exercise with many clubs operating throughout the year. However, everyday opportunities for walking are often overlooked. It is not necessary to drive everywhere!

Weight training

Non-aerobic exercise, designed to build up strength. Though stamina can also be improved if low weights are used with many repetitions.

	Strength	Suppleness	Stamina	Social
Badminton	●●	●●	●●	●●
Bowling	●	●	●	●●●
Cycling	●●	●	●●●	●
Dance	●●	●●	●	●●●
Exercise classes	●●●	●●●	●●●	●
Golf	●	●	●	●●●
Jogging	●●	●	●●●	●
Squash	●●	●●	●●●	●●
Swimming	●●●	●●●	●●●	●
Tennis	●●	●●	●●	●●
Team games	●●	●●	●●	●●●

Figure 9.1 Some popular exercises with ratings for fitness and sociability

Most sports centres provide weight facilities, and they can easily be provided within companies because they take up little space and are reasonably low cost items. However, good training is essential to minimise the risk of strains and injuries.

Yoga

A combination of posture and breathing exercises which is part of Hindu religious practice, and now popular in the West. Yoga can be provided in companies, requiring good instruction but no special facilities. Yoga is not aerobic and provides no benefit for stamina, but strengthens muscles and is good for suppleness. Yoga is as important for its benefits to the mind as to the body, providing an opportunity to meditate and relax.

Figure 9.1 summarises the fitness ratings for some of these exercises, and also gives them a rating for 'sociability'.

Exercising the workforce

So how are the benefits of fitness introduced to a group of employees? How should exercise be included in a corporate healthcare programme? To answer these questions it is necessary to consider current attitudes to exercise in Great Britain. A number of surveys of this subject have been undertaken for particular groups or areas, for example the Dumfries and Galloway Health Board included questions about exercise in an extensive study designed to provide a basis for developing health promotion programmes.

The questions were intended to find how much exercise people actually take. In fact the majority of those questioned (79 per cent) said that most of their time was taken up with at least moderate activity such as walking or housework. However, in the 18–44 age group, only 2 per cent of women said that their activity was vigorous. Twenty-eight per cent of men and 20 per cent of women in this age group were sedentary for most of the time. The survey asked how often people participated in aerobic exercise and found dramatic differences between the age groups. In the 18–44 age group, 40 per cent of males and 30 per cent of females engage in vigorous sport at least one day per week. But in the 45–64 age group, the figures for vigorous sport have declined to 10 per cent of males and 1 per cent of females.

These answers are useful because one of the major challenges for those promoting health at work is to avoid preaching to the converted. All organisations who have gone to the expense of installing fitness facilities at work have experienced the same phenomenon. It is that the facilities are immediately used by those who are already fit – they would have exercised anyway, and they have merely switched gratefully to the new, convenient location. So it is clear that, to switch non-exercisers to exercisers, publicity and encouragement will need to be especially directed towards the middle-aged, and perhaps particularly to women. This may be a matter not just of publicity, but of sensitivity. The middle-aged may not particularly wish to exercise with the young – and women may not wish to exercise with men. So it could be worthwhile copying the approach of most sports centres and gyms, and having sessions devoted to particular age groups and sexes. But do they want to start exercising? The Dumfries and Galloway survey also asked whether people thought they were taking enough exercise.

The survey results clearly showed that very many people feel they should exercise more. Overall, 40 per cent of men and 49 per cent of women felt that they did not take enough exercise. In both sexes, professional and white collar groups felt this most strongly, with more than 50 per cent of both sexes saying they did not exercise enough. Very importantly, three main reasons were selected for this lack of exercise – and all three can be addressed by employers. In priority order they were:

- lack of time;
- lack of incentive;
- lack of facilities.

The Dumfries and Galloway survey did not provide information about what sports were actually pursued, though other studies have looked at this. For example, the UK General Household Survey showed that walking was the most popular physical activity – indeed only 17 per cent participated in any other outdoor activity. Of the most popular sports some, such as fishing, darts and snooker, involve very little physical activity. The survey confirms other findings that participation rates are higher for men than for women, and that participation falls off sharply with age. It also shows that, while professional groups feel most strongly that they do not exercise enough, they are also the group which actually exercises most. This and similar surveys seem to show that no more than about 30 per cent of men, and 20 per cent of women engage in sufficiently vigorous activity to help protect them from heart disease.

Some other survey information which offers relevant information for devising corporate programmes is given in the analysis of the 'Getting In Shape' project. This started in 1983, and was a project publicised by the Sunday Times and run by the Sports Council and the Health

Education Council. It monitored almost two hundred people who pursued intensive exercise programmes, with a view to finding out what motivated them, what benefits they achieved, and how aerobic exercise compared with anaerobic exercise. The project showed convincingly that it was quite possible for average, middle-aged sedentary people to achieve high levels of fitness with about two hours exercise per week. Motivation to start the training, and to continue once started, was expressed in a variety of ways, but seems to have been based on a personal commitment and determination to become fit, together with the enjoyment of being with others in the group. The study report was reluctant to pronounce judgement on 'aerobic vs anaerobic' training, instead taking a 'horses for courses' view. In other words, both exercise types will improve 'fitness', and it is a matter of choosing what sort of activity you would like to improve at. However, it was clear that the aerobic exercises such as running, cycling, etc., had been found to be much more enjoyable and less boring than anaerobic exercises such as weight training. The overall conclusion was that, almost without exception, the improved fitness had made a real, beneficial contribution to everyday living. Participants reported improved alertness and stamina, and resources to cope with everyday life more easily than before.

In summary then, for the employer to successfully encourage employees to become fitter, it is desirable to provide at least some of the following:

- facilities, or access to facilities which enable regular exercising to be convenient;
- instruction in the correct way to exercise without harm or injury;
- testing of fitness before and during exercise to set safe targets and to monitor progress;
- time for employees to exercise without seriously eroding other activities;
- motivation in the form of awards, encouragement, publicity, and organisation of team activities;
- segregation for those who wish to exercise with people of their own age or sex;
- information about the huge range of exercises available, and the benefits to health of regular participation.

Health facilities in organisations

As mentioned earlier, some organisations have the budget and the space to provide physical facilities for exercise at the workplace. This is perhaps the ideal way to introduce the value of exercise to employees, and is a demonstration of true commitment by the employer. However, all of the above considerations should be applied or else the facilities will only be used by the already fit. Exercise facilities are a marvellous benefit, but must be accompanied by a programme of information and encouragement to ensure widespread use.

Facilities can easily expand to fill the available budget. There will be no difficulty spending millions of pounds on a swimming pool, squash courts, weight rooms – not to mention the associated saunas, solaria and jacuzzis! However, for all but a very few employers, such facilities are out of the question and the need is to make the most of a more modest budget. For a start, space alone will meet some needs, and would allow people to exercise before or after work, and during lunch breaks. To be properly used, there will also need to be somewhere to change and to shower.

Equipment can then be added, much at low cost – some very sophisticated and expensive. A good start might be an exercise bicycle and a rowing machine. For more ambitious projects, there are specialist companies which will take over all or any of the planning and installation stages. Whatever the facility, it is essential to support it with appropriate training. The providers of exercise equipment in companies all give training in correct use. This should become the responsibility of a specific individual in the company, who must ensure that the instruction is given to all others using the equipment.

Employers who would like to offer exercise facilities but cannot, might be able to negotiate special arrangements for their staff with local health clubs. There is an additional social benefit with such arrangements, as employees will get together to visit the facilities, and will certainly take an interest in each other's progress to fitness.

This checklist is a reminder of the actions which organisations can take to introduce the benefits of exercise to their employees:

- Does the nature of people's work provide good levels of exercise naturally, or is the work essentially sedentary with a need for exercise opportunities to be introduced?
- Do we provide information in the workplace about the benefits of being fit, and the options available for exercise?
- Is someone at work trained to give advice about exercise, and to give instruction on the use of exercise equipment, etc?
- Do we provide any exercise facilities for the use of employees?
- Do we have space in the workplace which could be made available for employees who wish to exercise?
- Do we encourage sporting activities by sponsorship, organisation of sports clubs, etc?
- Do our senior managers set an example by keeping fit, and encouraging their staff to exercise?
- Do we provide fitness testing so that employees can establish their level of fitness, their needs for exercise, and can monitor their progress?
- Are specific periods of time set aside for employees to exercise?
- Do we have any arrangements with local sports centres or health clubs to offer exercise facilities to employees?

CHAPTER 10
Health Education

Many organisations give a low profile to health education. Even where there is some activity, it often lacks the clarity of objectives and the properly managed approach which are necessary for success.

Health education has much in common with other activities in which the aim is to inform and persuade. It is often the 'campaign' approach – in which one means of communication actively reinforces the effect of the others – which proves most successful in raising awareness and changing behaviour.

The importance of health education for the employer is highlighted by the finding that much ill health could be prevented by changes in people's lifestyle. While these changes are unquestionably the individual's own responsibility, the fact that the average person spends most of his or her waking life at work means that no one is better placed than the employer to influence the process.

People are unlikely to take action unless they are not only fully informed but also motivated to do so – effective health education should therefore be seen as an essential part of an employee healthcare programme.

Introduction

Health education could be said to be one of the greatest missed opportunities of our day. The words themselves do not conjure up the sort of positive images likely to appeal to dynamic and successful managers. What many organisations do by way of health education – if they do anything at all – tends to be limited to anti-smoking posters with curling edges stuck up in the health centre waiting room, or a few unexciting leaflets to be dished out to anyone who is interested. This misses the whole point – which is not just about awareness but also about action – and represents a failure to seize an opportunity, which if taken would help people do something which could measurably improve their current health and their life expectancy.

Foundations

The vital importance of health education is based on a simple fact: people can make changes to the way they live which will improve not only the likely length but also the quality of their lives. This may be by changing what they eat, how much they exercise, their smoking habits or even the job they do. For this process to take place, a number of things need to happen. Firstly, there needs to be an awareness of the link between what they do and their health, and there are many leaflets, posters, films and videos whose purpose is to help increase this awareness.

But where so much health education of the leaflet and poster sort goes wrong is that it does not take people to the next stage, that of changing their behaviour and lifestyle. In short, they should do something differently as a result of the new awareness they have gained. Clearly, as in any other situation in which we are seeking to influence people's behaviour, there needs to be more than just information. Motivation is essential too. People have got to feel a strong enough incentive to take some action which may – as in the case of giving up smoking – be difficult, slow and uncomfortable.

In the remainder of this chapter, we look at some of the ways in which we can not only create awareness of health issues, but also take people onto the stage at which they modify their lifestyle and improve their health as a result. But first it is essential to explore the assumption that it is possible to improve our health by what we do. For if it is true, the implication is that health education should be a major thrust of any corporate healthcare programme. If it is false, then health education is a waste of time and money.

The case for health education

In Chapter 3, we quoted Government information which identifies the principal causes of premature death in the UK, and in particular:

- coronary heart disease;
- cerebrovascular disease (stroke);
- motor accidents;
- respiratory disease;
- lung cancer;
- breast cancer.

Looking at these in turn, it becomes clear that lifestyle is a major factor and that there is action the ordinary person can take to reduce the risk of disabling disease and premature death.

Coronary heart disease (CHD)

In view of the importance of CHD not only in the UK, but in the whole of the industrialised West, it is unsurprising that considerable research has gone into the factors which make CHD more likely, and we mentioned the main ones in Chapter 3:

- age;
- blood cholesterol level;
- blood pressure;
- cigarette smoking;
- diabetes;
- family history;
- lack of exercise;
- obesity;
- sex;
- stress.

Clearly, there is nothing we can do to change the fact that a close relative died of a heart attack or that we are male as opposed to female. But if we do have these fixed risk factors, it makes controlling the others even more important.

With most of the above, there is something the individual can do to reduce the risk, for:

- we can influence (to some extent) our blood cholesterol level;
- we can control (to some extent) blood pressure;
- we can choose not to smoke;
- we can decide to alter the amount and type of exercise we do;
- we can lose weight;
- we may be able to reduce the pressures placed on us, and we can certainly increase our ability to cope with them.

It is also clear from the research that these factors interact with each other. One of the findings of the Framingham study, mentioned in Chapter 3, was that a middle-aged man who not only smokes cigarettes but who also has raised blood cholesterol and raised blood pressure is about eight times more likely to suffer CHD than someone without these risk factors. Conversely, by encouraging people to take action to deal with more than one risk factor, a far more significant risk reduction can be achieved than by focusing on just one aspect – such as blood pressure – alone.

Although there is still more work to be done – especially to understand more fully how one factor interacts with one or more others – our understanding of these risk factors is now so well developed that computer programs have been written which will show the statistical probability of someone suffering from heart disease, either within a specified timescale – e.g. the next ten years – or by a certain age.

Far more importantly, these programs can be used interactively as a health education tool to counsel people and to demonstrate to them:

- what their risk factors are;
- how changes to their lifestyle would affect the risk level (see Figure 10.1);
- (where a series of visits takes place) what progress they have made since the last visit.

This approach, which is tailored to the individual, and which involves him or her, is far more likely to be successful than the traditional 'give up smoking – it's bad for your heart' lecture, no matter how true that particular message might be.

Cerebrovascular disease (stroke)

As we saw in Chapter 3, this disease has much in common with CHD, the essential difference being that we are talking about the blood supply to the brain rather than the blood supply to the heart muscle. As the two have so much in common, it is not surprising that the risk factors for CHD are also risk factors for cerebrovascular disease.

If this is the case, taking action to reduce CHD risk factors will simultaneously reduce the risk of stroke.

Motor accidents

This is especially a problem for the young, with road accidents being the most common cause of death in the 5–24 years age group. It is clearly a public safety issue and one which has been recognised by successive governments – hence the amount of effort that goes into road safety campaigns and the changes to the law which have required better training for one of the highest risk groups – motor-cyclists.

But it is also an issue for employers, and not just in relation to young members of a manager's family driving his or her company car. A number of companies have accepted that the greatest risk of fatal injury to their staff while at work is not the workplace itself, but driving. As

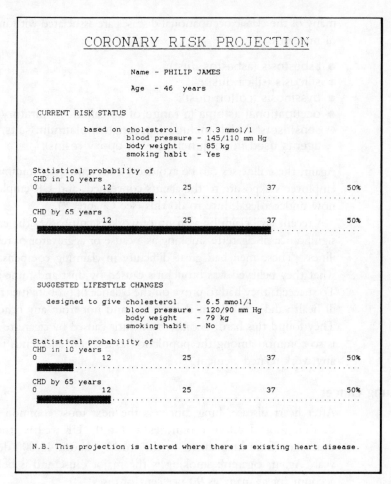

```
                CORONARY  RISK  PROJECTION


                      Name  -  PHILIP  JAMES

                      Age   -  46  years


        CURRENT RISK STATUS

            based on cholesterol    - 7.3 mmol/l
                      blood pressure - 145/110 mm Hg
                      body weight    - 85 kg
                      smoking habit  - Yes

        Statistical probability of
        CHD in 10 years
        0          12              25              37         50%


        CHD by 65 years
        0          12              25              37         50%



        SUGGESTED LIFESTYLE CHANGES

            designed to give cholesterol    - 6.5 mmol/l
                            blood pressure  - 120/90 mm Hg
                            body weight     - 79 kg
                            smoking habit   - No

        Statistical probability of
        CHD in 10 years
        0          12              25              37         50%


        CHD by 65 years
        0          12              25              37         50%



        N.B. This projection is altered where there is existing heart disease.
```

Figure 10.1 Coronary risk projection

a result they are seeking to protect their staff as well as possible, notably by the provision of defensive driving courses.

Respiratory disease

This includes a number of conditions such as bronchitis and emphysema which collectively represent the third most important cause of death in most developed countries – after heart disease and lung cancer. The answer to the question 'how far are they avoidable?' depends on the cause. One of the most significant of these is cigarette smoking – which is, as discussed above in the context of heart disease, an avoidable risk factor.

Respiratory disease may also result from occupational exposure, for many of the classic occupational diseases are associated with inhalation of materials:

- asbestosis (asbestos dust);
- silicosis (silica dust);
- byssinosis (cotton dust);
- occupational asthma (a range of so-called 'respiratory sensitisers' which include isocyanates, platinum salts, curing agents used in conjunction with epoxy resins).

Again, these illnesses can be avoided by preventing or minimising the employee's exposure to the agents concerned, and UK employers are now under a legal duty to do this (see Chapter 2).

A recent civil claim by a group of workers emphasises the enormous significance of cigarette smoking as a cause or aggravator of respiratory illness. These men had great difficulty in claiming compensation for what they believed was bronchitis caused by dust and fume at work. To succeed, they had to prove on the balance of probabilities that their ill health did result from their work, and not from any other factor. They found this hard, because bronchitis caused by cigarette smoking is so common among the population as a whole and tends to 'mask' any work-related element.

Lung cancer

After heart disease, lung cancer is the next most common cause of death in most developed countries, and in the UK we have the highest death rate from lung cancer in the world – about 40,000 deaths per year. Again, cigarette smoking is the major cause and is believed to account for as many as 90 per cent of cases.

Breast cancer

Breast cancer stands apart from the other causes of death discussed above in that its causes are not well-understood, and it is hence impossible to identify actions which the individual can take to minimise her risk level. However (and the point is equally valid for cervical cancer), health education has a vital role to play in the early detection of disease, notably through showing women how to examine their breasts for lumps and encouraging them to be aware of the significance of abnormalities such as discharge from the nipple. Without doubt, early detection significantly reduces the risk of developing serious illness.

We can draw the following conclusions from this review of the main causes of premature death:

- for all of them except breast cancer, the factors that are

- associated with increased risk are well-researched and documented;
- this is especially true for the two main causes of premature death, heart disease and lung cancer;
- it is possible for people to take action which will affect their risk level, so effective health education must make an important contribution to better health;
- some risk factors are relevant to more than one cause of death. For example, the person who has untreated high blood pressure is more likely to suffer from heart disease than the person with normal blood pressure. At the same time, he or she is more likely to have a stroke;
- cigarette smoking is such a significant factor in its own right that action to encourage people to reduce or stop smoking must be a priority;
- even where we cannot reduce the risk level, health education can help people identify problems at the early stages, at which treatment is most likely to be easy and effective.

There is therefore little doubt that health education is extremely valuable, and indeed should be a fundamental part of a corporate healthcare programme. The lives people lead do make a difference to their health, and if we can help them understand the link between the two, they are then better placed to make decisions which will improve their quality of life and their life expectancy.

Having established the case for 'why have effective health education', we need to look at the 'how'. But first, we need to deal with an obstacle that hinders many people's understanding of these issues. We will call this obstacle 'the myth of Auntie Gillian and Uncle John'.

The myth of Auntie Gillian and Uncle John

Many health educators have had the experience of counselling an individual, or indeed of talking to a group, when Auntie Gillian or Uncle John's case history is brought up:

'Auntie Gillian – now there's someone who knew how to live! She smoked 30 a day all her life, ate fried bread and dripping for breakfast and chips for dinner and tea, could put away a drink or two, and never took any exercise other than walking ten yards to the corner shop to get her paper.

Now there's a prime candidate for an early heart attack if what you're saying is right, yet she died peacefully in her sleep at the age of 91.'

Uncle John is the other side of the coin:

'What a miserable old soul Uncle John was. Lived an upright life, never smoked nor touched a drop of the hard stuff. Fanatic for exercise, up at the crack of dawn, pounding away on his exercise bike, lived on salad, yet look at him! Keels over with a heart attack on his 35th birthday and is dead before they could get him in the ambulance.

So what chance do I stand? I might as well carry on as I am if that's all the good healthy living would do me.'

The basic error behind both these accounts is that of inferring a general truth from a single specific case. But those involved in health education, and indeed in healthcare programmes in general, need to remember that all we know about risk factors and so forth is in terms of probabilities, not absolutes. The research on which our knowledge is based looks at large groups or 'populations' and we have to be very careful to remember the variations that occur whenever we study a large group of people.

There is no doubt that asbestos is bad for people's health, and yet there are cases of people who have been exposed to very high levels over a long period and appear to have suffered no ill effects. Equally, there are cases of comparatively low exposure – as in one case where a wife was only exposed to the asbestos dust her husband brought home on his overalls – which have nevertheless resulted in fatal illness.

Similarly with noise – expose a group of 100 workers to high noise levels for 10 years and you can predict the likely average deterioration in their ability to hear as they suffer from noise-induced hearing loss. Yet there will be some who suffer an unexpectedly high degree of deafness, while at the other end of the scale, there will be a group who seem almost immune. Unfortunately, there is no way of knowing who will fall into each of these categories.

Again, in spite of the weight of evidence about the dangers of smoking cigarettes, we cannot say to a heavy smoker that he or she will definitely suffer from heart disease or bronchitis – all we can say is that he or she is 'much more likely to' than a non-smoker, and we should also be able to give a scale of the comparative risk (how much more likely). So, we must be aware of individual variations, and remember that we are dealing with well-documented probabilities – not certainties.

The other key element is that we must be sure that the message we are putting over is the right one. Even a slight misunderstanding can have results which are potentially very serious. This is illustrated by a recent research study into why the take-up rate for NHS cervical smear tests is not higher. The study showed that many women avoid having cervical smear tests because they think a positive result means they have got cancer. This is a complete misunderstanding, because what the test is primarily looking for is pre-cancerous cells – i.e. the state before cancer has developed. Nevertheless the misunderstanding is widespread and is prejudicing the effectiveness of the NHS screening programme in detecting the problem early enough for treatment to have a high chance of success.

We must also be aware of the tremendous publicity that health issues currently receive. Hardly a week passes without the newspapers reporting the results of some new study which suggests a link between some aspect of diet/lifestyle and ill health. Many people find this flood of information at best confusing and at worst contradictory. Their reaction 'everything seems to be bad for you – so it doesn't really matter what I do' is understandable but extremely dangerous. One of the major functions of effective health education is to set the record straight and get these risks in perspective.

Having registered these concerns, let us explore some of the basic principles of health education.

Health education – the basic principles

The remainder of this chapter is based on two assumptions:

- this book's readers may not be personally involved in the delivery of health education, but they could be involved in the management of health education as one component within a healthcare programme, and therefore need an overview of the basic principles and techniques. They will also wish to be aware of external sources of materials and advice;
- health education is not fundamentally different from any other type of activity in which we are seeking to inform and persuade. Hence in seeking to make our health education programmes as effective as possible, we can draw not only on the experience of successful health education programmes, but on the wider field of effective business communication.

Six basic principles should be kept in mind at each stage of the planning and implementation of a health education programme:

1. HEALTH EDUCATION SHOULD RESPECT THE INDIVIDUAL

Health education is not a process in which a holier-than-thou medical elite tell the ignorant lay people how to live their lives. We are all responsible for ourselves, and for the choices we make that affect all aspects of our lives, including our health.

Health education is concerned with making sure that people:

- are aware that they do have choices and that the choices they make affect their health;
- make their choices on the basis of the best available evidence.

Obviously no health educator wants people to pursue a lifestyle which is likely to adversely affect their health, and will use his or her best efforts to persuade them otherwise. But ultimately, everyone has to make their own choices, and that should be respected.

The only exception to this is where the action individuals take puts not only themselves but also other people at risk. It is of course exactly this issue which is at the heart of the debate about passive smoking at work, as was discussed in Chapter 8.

2. HEALTH EDUCATION SHOULD BE PLANNED

Putting a few posters on the wall and dishing out health education leaflets is haphazard and likely to achieve very little. If we are serious about health education (and the evidence about the potential contribution health education could make to better health says we should be) we should plan it properly. This is dealt with in greater detail later in the chapter, but includes:

- having a clear objective (what are we trying to achieve by doing this?);
- being clear about the audience (who are we seeking to influence?);
- including some monitoring mechanism (how will we know whether we have been effective, so that we can change the approach if necessary?);
- allocating the proper resources (what time, money, personnel and facilities are needed?).

3. HEALTH EDUCATION SHOULD ADDRESS A REAL NEED

Evidence from successful health education programmes suggests that the best approach is to be as specific as possible as to campaign theme and the target audience.

The two main pointers to the priorities are:

- national statistics as to the main causes of preventable, premature death (since these indicate where the greatest scope for healthier lifestyles lies);
- what the target audience wants (since it is much easier to gain people's involvement if you are dealing with something which is already a genuine concern to them).

One area of health education which has been dramatically 'customer led' has been the provision of information about AIDS. In the late 1980s, so much interest and concern was generated about the risks of AIDS that many employers felt compelled to take action – both to put the situation in perspective and to reassure employees that the risk of contracting at work what is predominantly a sexually-transmitted disease is extremely slight.

4. EFFECTIVE HEALTH EDUCATION LEADS TO ACTION

Increasing awareness and conveying knowledge are of limited use by themselves. As with training in general, the acid test is whether people change their behaviour as a result. An effective programme will include not only the raising of awareness but also motivation to do something differently as a result. Some means of monitoring and re-inforcing these changes must also be included.

5. EFFECTIVE HEALTH EDUCATION PROBABLY INVOLVES USING A VARIETY OF MEDIA

Research done on safety publicity shows that using one medium on its own is comparatively unsuccessful. For example, where posters are used to create awareness or pass on information, they are of limited use on their own and quickly become 'part of the wallpaper' and lose their impact. Where they form part of an integrated campaign – reinforced by, for example, talks, questionnaires, demonstrations, give-aways, competitions – the effect is likely to be much greater.

The campaign approach also provides a way of creating a sustained interest and of avoiding a feeling of 'flavour of the month'. In this context it is important to emphasise that, just as the different elements of a health education campaign can be used to reinforce each other, so can exactly the opposite take place where an integrated approach is not adopted. The classic example of this is the healthy eating campaign which encourages people to eat a good diet and yet which is undermined by the fact that no one takes the trouble to ensure that the recommended healthy foods are available in the site restaurant.

6. HEALTH EDUCATION SHOULD BE CONSTRUCTIVE

Research suggests that health education materials designed to frighten individuals out of a certain lifestyle tend to shock them into inaction. Portrayal of the positive aspects of the new lifestyle is far more effective.

Planning health education

In *Promoting Health – a Practical Guide to Health Education*, Ewles and Simnett identified a number of stages as the essential elements of an effective health education programme, and these provide a useful checklist for the personnel manager who wishes to ensure that a proposed health education programme has been properly planned and thought through (see Figure 10.2).

The evaluation stage (which is often omitted) is vital and will provide information which can be fed back into each of the other stages.

Media

As noted above, an effective health education programme is likely to involve not one but several media, each reinforcing and building on the effect of the others.

Leaflets

Numerous leaflets are available on a wide range of health topics. Copies are available from the Health Education Authority and specialist bodies such as the Coronary Prevention Group. They are usually well-researched and illustrated, and written in an easy-to-read style. They are especially useful where someone wants information on a specific topic and as a reminder of the main points discussed at, say, a health education session.

Posters

Excellent posters are available from bodies such as the Health Education Authority and others. As stressed above, posters are

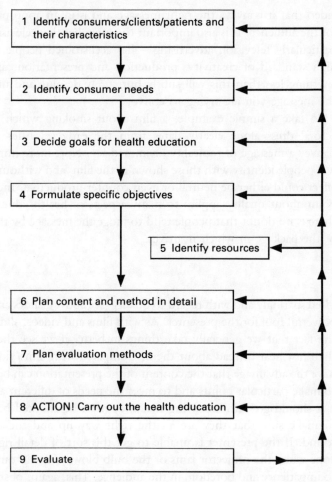

1 Identify consumers/clients/patients and their characteristics

2 Identify consumer needs

3 Decide goals for health education

4 Formulate specific objectives

5 Identify resources

6 Plan content and method in detail

7 Plan evaluation methods

8 ACTION! Carry out the health education

9 Evaluate

Source: Ewles and Simnett, 1985

Figure 10.2 Essential stages in an effective health education programme

unlikely to be effective when used in isolation, but can be a powerful component of a properly planned awareness campaign. They should be changed regularly as there is otherwise a danger of them becoming just 'part of the wallpaper'. They should also be removed if damaged – a tatty poster conveys a powerful subliminal message that the poster's theme is unimportant.

Films and videos

These are powerful communication tools. Since what they say cannot be altered, it is necessary to be sure before using a particular film or video that it conveys the right message and is in an appropriate style for the audience. It is also important to remember that television – and particularly television advertising – has accustomed people to a very high standard of creativity, production and presentation, and hence anything less than this will subtly but surely devalue and undermine the message you are trying to convey.

To take a simple example, a film about smoking which from the actors' dress alone clearly dates from the early seventies does not convey a message of topicality or immediacy. Nor, more importantly, will people identify with those shown in the film, and without this, the effect could either be neutral or even counter-productive. Indeed, this point about quality applies to many aspects of health education, for there is no doubt that people tend to judge the message by the quality of the package in which it arrives.

Slides

Used sparingly and with regard to quality (see above), slides are another powerful tool for the presenter. As with films and videos, slides exploit the fact that we generally take things in better if we see them rather than just hear or read about them. Compared with films/videos, they have the advantage that the content of the presentation can be adjusted to make particular points and to meet the needs of different audiences.

It should go without saying that they must be checked beforehand to make sure that they are all the right way up and the right way round. If the presenter is unable to get this sort of detail right – and cope when the projector jams or the bulb blows – it will quickly lead to impatience and boredom in the audience. This, again, obstructs and undermines the message we are seeking to convey.

Demonstrations

In health education it is impossible to avoid *some* technical detail and demonstrations can be a huge help in helping get round this potential obstacle to understanding and acceptance of the message. They can be used to turn abstract concepts into something concrete and readily understandable. Examples include a display showing what one unit of alcohol is depending on the drink involved, and using a carbon monoxide analyser to demonstrate the amount of carbon monoxide exhaled by a smoker. Demonstrations also have a particular value in reducing the mystique which often surrounds medical matters. They can be extremely persuasive and very memorable!

Questionnaires

As well as being a useful way of gathering information (e.g. how would employees feel about some proposed changes in the company smoking policy?), questionnaires can be used as a means of raising awareness and of gaining involvement.

Quizzes

Most people have some competitive streak and quizzes (preferably with a prize that people really want to win) are an excellent way of harnessing this. They get people involved and are a subtle way of stressing points made through some other medium (e.g. the quiz might include some questions that relate to a video shown earlier).

Give-aways

These are another useful way of re-inforcing a point made by some other means – pens, key fobs and note pads with a health education message are common examples. One problem with give-aways is that they need to be reasonably cheap, but if they are of poor quality there is the danger mentioned above of the medium undermining instead of supporting the message. The ideal give-away is therefore something cheap but of high perceived value.

We have placed particular stress on the desirability of using not one but several methods of conveying information and influencing attitudes – with each method re-inforcing the others. The following example of a successful health education evening formed part of a wider campaign to increase awareness of coronary heart disease and shows how this can work in practice.

The theme of the evening is 'Prevention of Coronary Heart Disease', the specific goals being to ensure that those attending understand what coronary heart disease is, and the factors under their control that make it more/less likely. Provide information that will inform and encourage people to adopt a healthier lifestyle.

The programme of events is as follows. Those attending are welcomed by the organisers and there follows a very short introductory talk explaining what the evening will cover, and a video is shown to introduce the topic and the concept of risk factors.

In an adjacent room, a number of practical 'stalls' have been set up, manned by suitably trained people. Each stall has relevant health education leaflets, which those attending are free to take away. Stall 1 is a computerised

---

stress assessment, which allows people to identify whether they are Personality Type A or B (see Chapter 6) and how far they are subject to stress. They receive a print out of their results and counselling is available to anyone who needs it.

Stall 2 allows people to have their blood pressure monitored, and again, advice is available where necessary.

Stall 3 is a simple fitness test, in which people climb onto and off a step of a set size (lower for women than for men) for a set time, after which their pulse rate is monitored. A simple questionnaire/consent form is completed first so that the organisers can identify anyone for whom the test might be dangerous.

Stall 4 consists of an instrument which allows people to monitor the carbon monoxide in their breath, this being a means of demonstrating to smokers the raised level of carboxyhaemoglobin (blood which is transporting carbon monoxide rather than oxygen) which they are likely to have.

Then follows a buffet, with the emphasis on healthy eating, during which people are given a quiz consisting of 10-15 questions on a sheet of paper, all the questions being concerned with coronary heart disease and its prevention. The correct answers are explained later and a prize given to the person with the best score.

Finally, a short slide show is used to show that a healthy lifestyle need not be dull and miserable, and to re-emphasise the key point of the evening – that many of the factors which make coronary heart disease more likely are under our direct control and we can therefore do something about them if we choose to.

Again it must be stressed that health education which goes no further than raising awareness is unlikely to achieve much. As with advertising, whose effectiveness is generally judged not by whether consumers gain awareness of the product but by whether they go out and buy it, health education needs to motivate people to action. Change does not happen simply from knowledge that change is a good thing – change has to be desired.

In the workplace, where we are dealing with groups of people, one powerful motivator is peer pressure. Hence if we can successfully involve groups in our health education, we are more likely to succeed. As was emphasised in Chapter 3, health screening can be tied in very powerfully with health education. It could be argued that every contact between an employee and occupational health staff is an opportunity for health education. Audiometry, for example, presents an ideal opportunity to talk further about noise-induced hearing loss, and the action the individual can take to safeguard his or her own hearing.

So health education should not be considered in isolation. It should be viewed as an integral part of an overall healthcare programme, the management of which is discussed in greater detail in the next chapter.

Sources of further information and advice

A number of bodies provide advisory services to help employers develop effective health education programmes, usually on a consultancy basis. The Health Education Authority provides a consultancy service of this kind, as do private companies such as AMI Healthcare, BUPA Occupational Health, GKN Occupational Health, Medisure and Minerva Health Management. A number of individuals have also set up consultancy services in this field.

Figure 10.3 gives details of some of the principal sources of health education materials:

Alcohol concern	071 833 3471
ASH (Action on Smoking and Health)	071 637 9843
BBC Training Videos	081 576 2361
British Heart Foundation	071 935 0185
Coronary Prevention Group	071 935 2889
Health Education Authority	071 383 3833
Health and Safety Executive	071 229 3456
HMSO	071 873 9090
Hotel and Catering Training Company	081 579 2400
Industrial Society	071 839 4300
Institute of Alcohol Studies	071 222 4001
Institute of Personnel Management	081 946 9100
National Back Pain Association	081 977 5474
National Rubella Council	071 837 0623
Noise Abatement Society	081 460 3146
Royal Society for the Prevention of Accidents	021 200 2461
Royal College of Nursing	071 409 3333
Scottish Health Education Group	031 447 8044
Scriptographic Publications	0420 541738
Terrence Higgins Trust	071 831 0330

Local Health Authorities (see phone book)
The Health Education Authority (see above) has compiled very useful lists of resources under various topic headings – e.g. smoking, heart disease, AIDS, occupational health.

Figure 10.3   Selected sources of health education materials

- Have the targets for health education been identified, both in terms of topics and audiences?
- Does our health education have clear objectives?
- Is it properly planned, and monitored to identify how far it has been successful?
- Is it properly resourced?
- Is a 'campaign' approach used so that one method reinforces another, or is there a series of isolated initiatives?
- Do we know where we can get suitable health education material to meet our needs?
- Are we open to new and interesting ways of putting over old messages?
- Are we careful to ensure that what we do as an organisation supports what we say in our health education?
- Have external specialists been invited to present ideas for health education programmes?
- Is health education integrated with other company training initiatives such as induction?

CHAPTER 11
Costs and Benefits

Corporate healthcare programmes can prove to be expensive when all elements of cost are taken into account. These include specialist fees, capital depreciation, and time costs of employees. However, careful monitoring and management of such costs will ensure that they are kept under control and that healthcare programmes are delivered to a budget.

Cost effectiveness is most likely to be achieved if clear objectives for the healthcare programme are set. The objectives should relate to real healthcare priorities, and be realistic and measurable. Progress towards objectives should be regularly reviewed, and used to obtain the commitment of the organisation and all its employees.

Healthcare programmes produce many benefits. Some of these are measurable and can be used to show cost savings. These include reductions in sickness absence and raised productivity. Other benefits are indirect, but are nevertheless the major motivation for many employers. They include the demonstration of real concern for the well-being of employees, and the raised enthusiasm and morale of a workforce committed to health.

Business managers are accustomed to making decisions on the basis of a single condition, namely financial performance. Investment in virtually anything is expected to show a return. Many organisations have strict criteria specifying the required rate of return before an investment can be made. So does corporate healthcare make financial sense?

Before setting up false expectations for this chapter, it must be said that the strict answer to the above question is usually 'don't know'. It is no more easy to spend the healthcare budget with certain knowledge that it will produce a return, than it is to spend the training budget, or the advertising budget. However, there is no doubt that corporate healthcare has the *potential* for saving more money than it

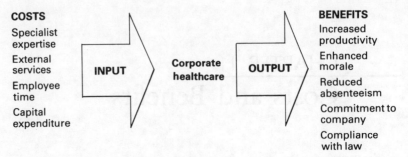

Figure 11.1 The costs and benefits of corporate healthcare can be presented as an input/output diagram

costs. There is also no doubt that some employment-based health schemes are a complete waste of money. This chapter considers the probable costs, the possible benefits, and the approaches most likely to ensure that the latter outweigh the former. Some major areas of cost and benefit are summarised in Figure 11.1.

The costs

Costs of healthcare programmes fall into a number of categories:

- employment costs of staff involved in the programme;
- employment costs of external specialists;
- capital equipment costs;
- cost of consumable items;
- time away from work while employees participate in the programme.

Staff costs are easy to underestimate. In-house specialists in healthcare are increasingly expensive to recruit and, to be effective, they need to maintain regular updating and training in new technology, legislation, techniques, etc. At least 15 per cent of their salary costs should be allocated to training, and subscription and purchase of specialist literature. As always, to their basic costs should be added the costs of support services – secretarial, personnel, etc. Again, these may be higher than the norm because their needs may be disproportionately high. If the service they provide involves a lot of personal contact, then making appointments, receiving people, etc. will be time-consuming. Also, many of the record keeping requirements are extremely onerous, requiring extensive back-up support. It is also worth noting that some of the back-up skills to healthcare providers are themselves specialist in nature. Examples are medical secretaries, and hygiene technicians.

Estimates of the staff costs necessary to support a corporate healthcare programme should include both direct and indirect costs. The direct costs are those discussed above, which relate directly to the specialist skills involved in the programme. The indirect costs are those of other personnel who become involved in circulating literature, arranging training, booking rooms, making appointments, analysing figures, preparing budgets, checking legal implications, and so on.

External specialists

External specialists may be involved in many aspects of corporate healthcare, and Chapter 5 reviewed the range of specialist skills which might be needed. Most specialists will be willing to arrange payment for their services in one of four ways:

1. A QUOTED DAILY OR HOURLY RATE

There is a wide range of professional charges depending upon level of skill required, complexity of the job, and location, but daily rates would typically be in the range of £400 to £800. This arrangement is straightforward, but open-ended if you do not know how long the work will take – and there is a motivation for the supplier to take as long as possible!

2. A PRICE FOR THE JOB

If the requirement is to undertake a specific assignment, such as a noise survey, a health screening programme, or a healthcare campaign, then specialists will be able to quote for undertaking that particular work. In many cases, this will be quite a formal process in which several quotes will be submitted in response to a tender specification. Provided the job can be clearly defined, this is a good approach since the cost of the work will be clearly understood in advance. However, it is *essential* to ensure that both parties know exactly what the job entails, and how its quality is to be assessed. If there is any ambiguity, there is likely to be conflict when the bill is presented.

3. A RETAINER

Specialists who provide a fairly regular service through the year, or who are 'on call' to respond to problems, are accustomed to providing services on a guaranteed retainer basis – probably a monthly fee which is paid whether they are used or not. If they are called on to provide service beyond that covered in the retainer, they will submit an additional bill for payment. This is a good way of retaining the services of someone who is likely to be regularly used. It commits them to the organisation, and avoids the need to prepare frequent invoices for small sums. Typical retainer arrangements would be with general practitioners who are available for occasional on-site service, routine telephone contact, and some level of pre-employment screening. The retainer arrangement might be £1000–2000 per year, with supplementary payments as appropriate.

4. A CONTRACT

A substantial level of service provided on a continuing basis, is likely to require a formal contract of service. Some externally-provided corporate healthcare programmes involve teams of specially recruited people servicing contracts valued at several hundred thousand pounds per annum. The contract will be a legally binding document which sets out the service to be provided, the fee and arrangements for its review and renewal, and the period of notice required for either party to terminate the arrangement.

Capital costs

Capital costs include all equipment purchase necessary to implement the corporate healthcare programme. Such programmes can run on the basis of virtually no capital requirements, through to enormous projects requiring new buildings and extensive facilities. However, the following checklist covers items which might typically be required:

- environmental control equipment such as dust extractors and acoustic booths;
- sampling and analysis equipment, such as noise meters, dust samplers, and gas detectors;
- furniture and fittings, such as desks and filing cabinets;
- medical equipment such as couches, spirometers, sphygmomanometers, blood analysers and audiometers;
- computers and printers to run screening programmes, store records, etc.;
- fitness equipment such as exercise bikes and rowing machines.

Building such costs into a budget will involve making assumptions about their rate of depreciation, and the organisation may have fixed procedures for doing this. Healthcare equipment can be subject to considerable wear and tear, and have little residual value after quite a short period. A reasonable assumption would be to write off most specialist items over about three years, though more accurate budgeting would require each item to be individually considered. It should also be borne in mind that repair and maintenance can be expensive, and the cost of maintenance contracts should be added to the budget.

Consumable costs

Consumable costs cover the disposable items which will be used during the healthcare programme. Typical costs include:

- stationery, postage and telephone costs;
- posters and publicity material;
- suitable clothing for nurses, etc.;
- protective clothing and replacement filters, etc.;
- reagents for laboratory and clinical tests;
- clinical disposables such as swabs and bandages.

Employee time

Employee time will vary according to the nature of the healthcare programme – and the generosity of the employer! Programmes for say, environmental improvement measures, need take up no employee time. On the other hand, education and training is likely to require participants to take time away from their work. Some health services offer the option of being provided either in or out of working time – for example exercise classes and health screening programmes. It is a fact of life that attendance is much higher for programmes run within working time. Some health education, particularly on work-related illnesses can be included in other, more general, training programmes. Costing of employee time may be straightforward because it has to be made up in paid overtime, or it may require an assumption that an employee not working costs, say, £10 per hour.

The benefits

Before itemising the benefits that might be obtained from corporate healthcare programmes, a word of caution should be introduced. This is because many organisations who are enthusiastically committed to promoting employee health, and who have no doubt that this is in their commercial interests, would be unable to quantify, or even clearly identify, the benefits. This is because the advantages are essentially intangible. They are reflected in concepts like 'commitment', 'quality', and 'care'. Before these ideas are dismissed as truisms, accepted without reason, it should be said that many business judgements rely on such qualitative assessments. Few companies could draw up the balance sheet for meeting the British Quality Standard, 5750, but the commitment to quality is a hallmark of the best and most successful businesses. In their famous book *In Search of Excellence*, Peters and Waterman identified characteristics which were shared by the USA's best run companies. They consistently found that good businesses achieved 'productivity through people', and that the companies that protected their most valuable asset – their people – had the best records of growth and financial performance. This was achieved without all staff benefits being queried to see if they produced a financial return – they were queried to see if they were real benefits.

However, there is no doubt that the money involved in corporate healthcare programmes is not all one way traffic. There is real potential for return, with the following items showing the greatest likelihood of savings:

- reduced absenteeism;
- reduced mortality;
- higher productivity;
- greater employee commitment;
- reduced medical costs.

Absenteeism

Absenteeism has been referred to many times in this book. It is perhaps *the* measure of employee health. It has also been noted how few companies fully measure and analyse sickness absence – even though they may rigorously analyse personnel records of much less importance. It is often quoted that illness is the cause of 30 times more absence than strikes, but because this is uniformly spread and has little drama, it is rarely publicised and often ignored. Healthcare programmes have consistently been shown to reduce absenteeism, and there seem to be three reasons for the effect. Firstly, the frequency of illness is reduced by improvements in employee health. Secondly, employees can return to work earlier after illness because the employer will be better able to provide support. Thirdly, non-genuine absence will be reduced because there will be more scrutiny of the reasons for illness.

The potential for saving is considerable. If the cost of absence is assumed to be a conservative £50 per day, and the sickness absence rate is assumed to be 5 per cent (also conservative), then the annual cost to a company with 1000 employees is almost £600,000. If this was reduced to the 2 per cent absence more common in Japan, the annual saving would be £360,000, or £360 per employee. If a decision was made to invest in absence reduction, but to require 100 per cent return on investment, then the question would be 'could healthcare expenditure of £180 per head per annum reduce sickness absence by 60 per cent?' Since such expenditure would justify several dedicated full time specialists, a sophisticated computer analysis and recording system, preventive health screening and employee welfare facilities, then it has to be concluded that there is at least a sporting chance.

Mortality

Mortality reduction is one of the aims of all healthcare programmes. To be strictly accurate, the aim is to reduce *premature* mortality, to ensure that people enjoy their full working lives, and commence a healthy retirement. The benefits to the employer are clear. Death in service and early medical retirement costs are high for both the pension fund and the employer. As well as the direct costs, employee recruitment and training costs are high and increasing, and the loss of a key employee can be almost unquantifiable. Some elements of such costs are illustrated in Figure 11.2. The major causes of premature death have been reviewed in a number of chapters, and will be priorities in most corporate healthcare programmes. They include coronary heart disease, breast cancer, strokes, lung cancer, motor accidents, and respiratory disease. Importantly, they can all be reduced by measures for prevention or early detection, at extremely low cost.

- external recruitment costs (advertising, agency costs, etc.)
- internal recruitment costs (interviewing, personnel admin., etc.)
- lost production during recruitment
- low productivity during training period
- training costs
- morale effect on organisation

Figure 11.2 Replacement costs of an employee

Studies to estimate the cost-effectiveness of programmes aimed at reducing mortality, recognised a weakness. It is that no allowance is made for the quality of the life that is saved. To overcome this, a commonly used yardstick to compare alternative programmes is the 'cost per QUALY'. A QUALY is a 'Quality Adjusted Life Year', in which the value of a life year gained is reduced in value if it falls below a year of perfect health. While there is still much work to be done on the subject of healthcare costing, it is extremely clear that preventive health programmes among working people represents outstanding value for money. A report by the Standing Medical Advisory Committee in 1990 considered the cost-effectiveness of opportunistic cholesterol testing, and used cost per QUALY estimates as the basis for comparing alternative health initiatives. Some typical figures are as follows:

Preventative health programme	Cost per quality adjusted life-year
Hospital haemodialysis for kidney failure	£19,000
Heart transplant	£6,900
Cervical/breast cancer screening	£5,500
Kidney transplant	£4,100
Cholesterol testing all adults 25–69 years	£2,852
Cholesterol testing all women 40–69 years	£2,602
Hip replacement	£1,030
Cholesterol testing all men 40–69 years	£871
Diet intervention only, women 40–69 years	£605
Cholesterol testing men with history of CHD, 40–69 years	£99
Diet intervention only, men 40–69 years	£44

These figures are part only of a complex study, and many other factors such as actual numbers of lives saved, have to be taken into account in deciding medical priorities. However, they do indicate the potential of preventive screening and education programmes for people at work – especially those with elevated health risk factors.

Productivity

Productivity improvements are likely to be achieved among people at work who receive healthcare services. These result both from the fact that healthy people work better, and from the 'Hawthorne Effect' – the observation by Elton Mayo that people work better when they see that the employer is taking an interest in them. In some cases, health programmes can be specifically targeted at productivity improvements. Examples would be eye testing for those whose jobs require visual acuity, and fitness testing and improvement for people who have to handle heavy loads. However, the real benefits to productivity are likely to be indirect and probably difficult to measure – they result from the greater alertness and enthusiasm of a workforce which is taking care of its health.

Commitment

Commitment of employees – to their work and to their employer – is a result of corporate health programmes, and has definite financial value. At its simplest level, this results from the addition of a 'perk' to the employment package and, in the perk stakes, healthcare ranks extremely high. It is possible to add sophisticated on-site health screening for all employees at relatively low cost – say £50 per head. As well as all the healthcare benefits this produces, it has far greater perceived value than the equivalent amount added to salary. As demographic shifts continue to reduce the availability of skilled personnel, there is growing need to offer an attractive employment 'package' to attract and keep good people. Health facilities serve the dual purpose of enhancing the package, and also demonstrating commitment to people. At a more fundamental level, employees do genuinely appreciate commitment from their employer, and respond with greater loyalty and co-operation. Investment in healthcare is rarely entirely mercenary, and includes a genuine desire by the employer to safeguard his employees – which they, in turn, appreciate.

Medical cost

Medical cost reduction has been the basis for nearly all financial analysis of corporate health programmes to date. However, the reason is that such studies have originated in the USA, where medical costs are invariably funded by the employer, and where such costs are relatively easy to monitor. The most closely examined programme is that run by Johnson and Johnson, who started the 'Live for Life' programme in 1979. This consists of a health screening assessment for each employee, coupled with counselling and the opportunity to participate in specific health programmes dealing with particular aspects of health such as smoking and stress. Live for Life participants have shown reductions in sickness absence, and in hospital inpatient costs, as compared with a control group. It is calculated that this results in a net saving for companies participating in the scheme.

Such results are of limited value for companies in Great Britain where cultural differences mean that results are not necessarily comparable, and where hospital costs are not usually paid directly by the employer. However, they could become increasingly relevant as more employers provide private health insurance and, as considered in Chapter 4, take on at least part of the risk funding. Meanwhile, the USA studies confirm some important points:

- that corporate healthcare does reduce illness;
- that health programmes for well people do provide ultimate cost-benefit;
- that health screening and education does result in a change to healthier lifestyles.

Most benefit for least cost

We have already observed that the debate over whether corporate health programmes save money, is continuing. The answer will undoubtedly be that some do and some don't. However, even those that don't may be worthwhile because they reduce ill health and premature death. Many employers accept this as a vital business objective – to be placed on the same level as making a profit and complying with the law. But the fact that employee healthcare is 'a good thing' is not a reason to throw money at it, and it is worth considering ways to ensure that any healthcare resource is allocated as effectively as possible. There are three essential principles: first, set objectives, then measure performance, and then shop around.

Objectives

Objectives are absolutely vital if healthcare programmes are to be worthwhile. In reviewing many company approaches to employee health, one observation stands out sharply – it is that companies achieve results if they *want* to achieve results. For example, if a company buys a no smoking programme because it seems reasonable value, and a good thing to do, it may or may not reduce the level of smoking in the workplace. But if the company declares an objective of cutting smoking by 25 per cent, and then finds ways of doing it, it is far more likely to produce results. Objectives, in healthcare as in everything else, should be challenging but attainable. Once achieved, new objectives can be set. Objectives are the key partly because they allow progress to be measured. As the Cheshire cat said to Alice in Wonderland, you won't know if you have made progress until you have decided where you want to go. Objectives are also essential because they establish *commitment* – they enable people to work towards goals.

Objectives need to come from within the organisation, and may be designed to address very specific circumstances or desires. But as a starting point for discussion, corporate healthcare objectives might take the following forms:

- reduce absenteeism by a defined percentage;
- statistically reduce coronary risk factors in employees by an agreed amount;
- fully comply with all aspects of the COSHH regulations;
- increase the number of employees taking regular exercise by a certain level;
- eliminate cases of noise-induced deafness;
- train a certain percentage of the workforce in basic first-aid procedures.

It follows, of course, that the corporate healthcare programme will then be designed and purchased to meet the objectives, rather than arbitrarily chosen with no clear purpose in mind. This will immediately rule out certain providers, and include others. It will also mean that providers can be given a clear brief showing what is expected of them.

It is particularly important to emphasise that healthcare objectives should be selected to meet *priorities*. There may well be pressing issues which can be tackled at low cost – perhaps a short training programme, or some aspects of environmental improvement – which will produce substantial benefits and be most appreciated by employees. If the health priorities are not obvious, then a period of assessment may be needed. This would involve gathering data, surveying opinions, testing the environment, etc., to give a basis for future planning.

Measurement

Measurement of results follows naturally from setting objectives. Indeed, a requirement in setting the objectives should be that their achievement can be measured. The measurement should be a defined responsibility, and this should be coupled with publicity for the achievements – through newsletters, staff magazines, notice boards, award presentations, etc. It is worth repeating that the measurement of ill-health, the cause of vast loss of production in Great Britain, is undertaken badly by nearly all organisations. So the measurement process may involve starting from scratch.

A starting point which will almost always be required is measurement and analysis of sickness absence. Accurate sickness absence records are essential, if only to ensure that the employer can reclaim the full SSP entitlement. This should ideally exist *before* the healthcare programme is started, to give a baseline against which progress can be measured. As stated previously, a good comparison is with the level of analysis which most companies give to accidents at work (partly because of the legal requirement to document accidents). Sickness absence should similarly be capable of analysis by:

- who is off sick;
- the duration of sickness absence;
- the cause of sickness absence;
- the location of those absent (building, department, etc.);
- the times of the absence (day of week, month, etc.);
- trends in sickness absence;
- absence according to age, sex, and job type.

Armed with such analysis, it is very much easier to decide on healthcare priorities, to devise action programmes, and to see if the programme is achieving results.

Careful selection

Shopping carefully is as worthwhile in corporate health as in anything else. As Chapter 5 showed, there is an enormous range of services, specialists, and provider organisations. Inevitably, they vary in the extent to which they offer value for money. However, shopping around will not necessarily mean always buying the cheapest service, since healthcare varies not just in price but in quality. The aim is therefore to find cost-effectiveness, rather than just cheapness. This is particularly true when buying consultancy and training services. The best consultants command the highest fees – but this is because they know their subject better, present their findings better and, at the end of the day, are more likely to achieve results than their cheaper counterparts. The following checklist is designed to help find value for money in buying services from external providers:

- Can they demonstrate convincing qualifications and experience in the necessary areas?
- Are they willing to set out exactly how their charges are broken down?
- Do they quickly understand what is wanted of them, and are they happy to work to defined objectives?
- Can they refer you to other satisfied customers?
- Do they have access to any necessary back-up facilities?
- Can they organise appropriate follow-up programmes when further needs are identified?
- Do they have enough faith in their own services to provide them for their own staff?
- Do they present themselves professionally and convincingly?
- Have you obtained proposals from a sufficient number of providers to give a good basis for comparison?

The above approach should ensure that the service is provided professionally and competitively; that it is set up to meet properly designed objectives; and that it has the best possible chance of achieving real results.

┌─ *CHECKLIST* ──┐

This checklist is designed to assist in introducing corporate healthcare programmes which produce a high level of benefits at realistic levels of expenditure:

- Have we set clear, measurable objectives for the proposed healthcare programme?
- Is there a good system of measurement in place, for example of sickness absence, to show current healthcare performance, and to demonstrate future improvements?
- Do we know the cost to the organisation of a day's sickness absence?
- Have all healthcare proposals been fully costed out – to include all employment costs, specialist costs, equipment costs, etc.?
- Have we obtained a sufficient number of external quotations to ensure that high-quality, competitively-priced services are being used?
- Have we presented all the benefits of healthcare programmes to employees and managers, and have all available publicity opportunities been used?
- Have all healthcare benefits been costed, so that they can be compared with the expenditure incurred?
- Have we set the budget for healthcare services, and are there defined procedures for controlling expenditure?
- Are there clear management responsibilities for running the corporate healthcare programme, for defining and reviewing objectives, and for achieving results?
- Have our health *priorities* been examined, to ensure that health expenditure is being directed to areas of greatest need?

└──┘

CHAPTER 12

The Management of Corporate Healthcare Programmes

Interest in health issues is running at an unprecedentedly high level and this is reflected in employees' raised expectations about the provision of healthcare services at work. At the same time, new concern about health hazards at work, together with new legislation and an awareness of the major causes of illness and premature death are compelling employers to look more closely at health issues.

There is no fundamental difference between managing an employee healthcare programme and managing any other sort of major project. There is the same need for careful planning, for winning the support and commitment of key people, and for the proper management of resources – people, time and money.

Above all, what is needed is a clear vision of what the organisation is seeking to achieve in its healthcare activities, translated into objectives which are clear and which are monitored.

The need for a plan

This book is based on the philosophy that corporate healthcare is too important to be done haphazardly or half-heartedly. Healthcare is most likely to be effective if it is properly planned and co-ordinated. Indeed, a fundamental argument of most of this book's chapters is that healthcare should be subject to exactly the same management disciplines as any other area of business activity.

Nothing should be done simply because 'it seemed like a good idea'. Organisations should be clear about what they are seeking to achieve and healthcare should be a reflection of a carefully thought-out commitment to what is involved – both in terms of the investment of resources and of the results expected. Objectives should be clearly defined, and the extent to which they are achieved should be monitored. In short, healthcare should not be something which exists in isolation – it should be programmed, and the programme should be managed, and that is what this chapter is about.

But first it is useful to stand back and look at the influences which are shaping both what organisations are doing in this field, and also what employees increasingly expect.

Key trends

Health high on the agenda

In society as a whole, health is now one of people's major preoccupations. It has become an industry in its own right. Millions of pounds' worth of products ranging from margarine to massage are sold by appealing to people's concern about health. Millions of words are written each year on health topics – it is hard to pick up a newspaper or magazine without reading about stress, blood pressure, cholesterol, health farms, health foods, fitness and so on.

Two other issues which are currently receiving great media attention – food safety and the environment – are themselves directly linked to health. In the workplace too, concern about health issues is at an unprecedentedly high level. Employees increasingly expect some sort of healthcare to be provided in their workplace, for example:

- provision of an occupational health service;
- availability of health screening;
- exercise facilities;
- stringent control of work-related health hazards, such as noise, dust and chemicals;
- stringent control of the working environment generally (heating, lighting, ventilation);
- control of smoking at work;
- availability of 'healthy' food in the staff restaurant or canteen;
- supportive policies on issues such as stress and alcohol;
- provision of health insurance as part of the benefits package.

New issues

At the same time, employees and managers are becoming aware of 'new' potential health at work problems. Is working with a VDU harmful to my health? A lot of people in the new office have been off work with coughs and colds recently – does this mean we've got a 'Sick

Building'? Am I at risk from repetitive strain injury? Are our water systems correctly maintained so as to prevent an outbreak of Legionnaire's disease? These are all searching and increasingly common questions.

As we have seen in Chapter 2, employers are subject to an increasing array of legal requirements concerned with the protection of the employee's health and safety at work. Few people with responsibilities for personnel management can have missed the fact that most of the recently introduced health and safety legislation is in fact concerned far more with health than with safety – for example the COSHH and Noise at Work Regulations.

Looking at what is in the pipeline, notably from the EC, it is clear that this trend will continue – with legislation planned on VDUs, manual handling and working conditions for pregnant women, to give but three examples. On the civil claims side, new awareness of work-related issues such as Repetitive Strain Injury (RSI) and noise-induced hearing loss brings with it not only a wider range of potential compensation claims, but also a greater willingness to put a claim in.

Evidence from companies suggests that employees are more ready than in the past to make health-related compensation claims. In one former heavy industry area, solicitors advertise on local radio, offering their services to 'help' anyone who thinks they may have noise-induced hearing loss make a successful claim. It is also likely that the new, more specific, statutory requirements – notably COSHH and the Noise at Work Regulations – will make health-related compensation claims easier to pursue successfully, because the action expected of the employer is spelt out in much more detail.

Occupational health – broader role

However, there is a further aspect which is probably of even greater significance: the expanding of occupational health's own horizons. While occupational health has always been concerned with the prevention of work-related health problems such as asbestosis or dermatitis, a new understanding has emerged of the need for a broader role.

Department of Health statistics paint a gloomy picture of millions of hours of productive life lost as a result of preventable premature death. As we have seen, the prime causes are heart disease and lung disease – both areas where the individual, properly counselled, can bring about a quantifiable reduction in his or her own risk. Most occupational health units are doing more work in this area, even if it does take them into 'difficult' areas such as employees' personal smoking, eating and exercise habits.

Health and the business

Finally, there is a trend towards a more business-driven approach to occupational health. It is likely that in the future occupational health services will work far more closely with other management disciplines than they do now, and in their turn, managers in general will become more involved with health issues. At the same time, the occupational health unit's contribution to the business will be better analysed and appreciated, and will be seen far more in cost/benefit terms.

As was highlighted in the last chapter, there is a shortage of information about the cost/benefits of improved corporate healthcare. The best-documented examples tend to come from the USA – notably the Johnson & Johnson 'Live for Life' campaign – where large employers pay the health insurance premiums for all their employees. They are hence much better placed to quantify the saving made when improved healthcare in the workplace leads to fewer claims and lower treatment costs, which in turn translates into lower insurance premiums for the employer.

However, it is likely that better information will emerge in the UK, and that healthcare services will increasingly be judged not only qualitatively but quantitively. Above all, the management disciplines of planning, objective-setting, prioritising, and monitoring will assert a greater influence over thinking in occupational health. In short, the management of occupational health will become far more strategic in character, and care programmes will be managed far more in terms of the results they can deliver.

A strategy for health at work

'Strategy' comes from the Greek 'strategos' meaning a general, or a supreme command such as a general's. In post-World War II military parlance, strategic denotes 'long range' as opposed to tactical or battlefield weapons, and this has been transferred into management thinking, with 'strategic planning' meaning 'long-term planning' and 'tactical planning' meaning 'short/medium-term planning'.

As the National Health Service is reorganised so that it is more market-driven, with patients as the consumers, hospitals as the providers and doctors assuming far greater budgetary responsibility, it is becoming clear that health professionals need management training. Equally, in the workplace occupational health unit, it is often the management skills which are lacking – the work being done is excellent from a preventive/caring viewpoint, but it lacks structure, objectives, clear priorities and performance indicators – that is, there is no strategy.

The management culture

Interestingly, nurses in industry often do not see themselves as managers, seeing an association with 'the management' as potentially threatening to their independence and to their professional relationship with their patients or 'clients'. Nor do managers see nurses as managers, although nurses' professional training and responsibilities are probably greater than those of many managers.

The occupational health nurse is often cut off from the mainstream of management, with occupational health seen as a peripheral and subordinate function somewhere in personnel. In very few companies do occupational health staff participate in management decision-making. They may suffer from reporting to someone who has no special knowledge of employee health issues nor vision of the full contribution occupational health could make to the business.

From the point of view of occupational health staff, working for an organisation outside the healthcare sector may well give them the anomaly of having no proper professional/clinical reporting line, and this may increase their defensiveness towards 'management'. Misunderstandings on both sides over confidentiality and other ethical issues may cause further friction. However, in the remainder of this chapter, we argue that workplace healthcare could benefit tremendously from the greater use of basic strategic management techniques, such as the following.

1. Planning

Many occupational health services in industry today do not not seem to have a well-developed plan. As a result the energies of those involved do not have a clear focus, nor are resources being used as effectively as they might be. Better planning and priority-setting would mean that healthcare programmes use resources more effectively, will be more likely to receive senior management endorsement and will also be more likely to succeed in attaining their objectives – simply through being better thought-out in the first place.

2. Setting standards

Clear standards will also help healthcare staff gain support for their programmes, and will give a clarity of purpose which is necessary for any successful endeavour and yet which is sometimes lacking from other-

LOOKING AFTER CORPORATE HEALTH

wise well-intentioned occupational health initiatives. This will include adequate training for occupational health staff, and encouraging those who do not yet have the appropriate professional qualifications to gain them.

3. Defining priorities

As the field of potential activity in occupational health becomes wider, it is important to set priorities – another basic management discipline. How easy it is to hide behind the myth that everything one does is important and therefore that it does not matter exactly how one's professional activity is channelled.

4. Talking costs and benefits

Occupational health is expensive. Trained staff of the right calibre are costly, as are medical equipment and supplies. Occupational health staff need to achieve a better understanding of costs and benefits and to be able to talk convincingly about these issues with other managers. This might involve, as mentioned in Chapter 11, looking closely at sickness absence and being able to demonstrate improvements resulting from particular occupational health programmes – and the resulting savings.

5. Using information technology

Exciting opportunities have opened up for the use of information technology in occupational health and there are many potential benefits. However, many healthcare staff do not feel comfortable with computers – presumably because of a lack of training/familiarisation opportunities. It is another basic management tool which occupational health staff would do well to get to grips with. Benefits could include more efficient organisation of records, improved analysis of data and better targeting of the unit's activity.

6. Monitoring results

Monitoring is a further management technique that will increasingly be applied in the occupational health sphere, possibly in the form of 'occupational health audits'. The concept is simple: having agreed objectives and priorities, it is then a basic management discipline to check how effective the implementation is, and this process usually provides valuable feedback which will enhance the end result. All managers are stewards of human and financial resources – and usually both. Any manager should therefore be ready to submit that stewardship to an objective audit.

Developing the plan

As was stressed at the beginning of this chapter, there is absolutely no reason why the planning process and management techniques applied to every other area of commercial activity cannot be applied to healthcare. This is not because they put everything on a financial footing – they don't – but because they work. While there are huge differences between, say, building a new factory, and launching a health screening or exercise programme, there is far more common ground – in terms of the elements essential for success – than would appear to be the case at first sight.

Equally, the approach outlined here is applicable not only to the major healthcare programme running over a number of years and costing many thousands of pounds. In a simplified form, it can be applied just as effectively to much smaller projects. There are six key elements: 1. assessment; 2. planning; 3. endorsement; 4. training; 5. implementation; 6. monitoring.

1. ASSESSMENT

The first stage has got to include a thorough assessment of what we are thinking of doing, and why we think it is a good idea. Essentially, this stage asks the question: where are we now, and where do we want to go to? Since most organisations will already have some sort of healthcare provision in place already, this should be looked at too. A number of questions should be asked, such as:

- what are its objectives?
- what does it cost?
- how successful is it?

But the most important aspect of this assessment is to identify the organisation's needs and aspirations. These may include such things as:

- we want to be seen as a caring and healthy employer;
- we want to attract and be able to keep high-calibre staff;
- we need a workforce which is not only skilled, but also highly motivated and productive;
- we would like to see absenteeism reduced from 4 to 2.5 per cent;
- we want to meet all relevant legal requirements, and if possible go beyond any minimum standard laid down by the law;
- we want to respond to employee's expectations and interest in health issues;

- we want to use resources more efficiently;
- we wish to reach the same excellence in our working environment and facilities as we achieve in the products we manufacture or the services we provide.

This stage may well involve detailed investigation of problems: do we have a sickness absence problem? What is it costing us? Do we have employees whose health is deteriorating because of stress, or because they drink too much? How many staff would use exercise facilities if they were provided? Would it just be those employees who are keen on exercise already? What would be the attitude towards workplace health screening?

This stage should also involve a lot of discussion, possibly involving some of the outside specialist services discussed in Chapter 5, and may be time-consuming. The checklists which appear in each chapter of this book should help structure the assessment process. This stage may turn up some unpleasant truths; it may also show where some aspect could be improved comparatively cheaply and easily, but at least by the end of it we should be developing clear ideas about the two key questions:

- what sort of healthcare provision do we as an organisation wish to make for our employees?
- what sort of resources are we going to have to put in to achieve that provision?

The process is illustrated in Figure 12.1.

2. PLANNING
Having obtained the overview, the next stage is to draw up the detailed strategy, and to develop much more specific answers to questions such as the following:

- what are our objectives – year one, year five, long-term?
- what are the priorities? No two organisations will have identical needs – what matters most to us?
- what resources are required – people, time, money?
- what timescale are we looking at, and is it realistic?
- how will we check progress against our objectives (the objectives must be framed in such as way as to allow this).

Particular thought should be given to defining the priorities, not only because of variations between organisations as mentioned above, but also because healthcare is a field in which there is an almost infinite range of things one could do. In practice, resources will be limited and therefore decisions have to be made about what is most worthwhile.

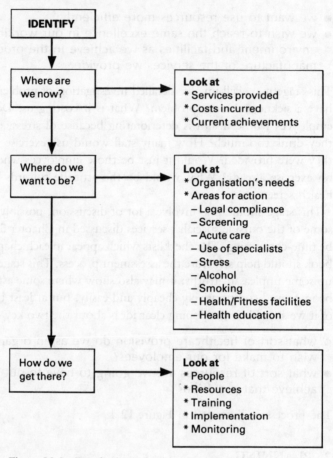

Figure 12.1 Developing a healthcare vision

As in any other field of management, it is essential that responsibilities are properly defined, so that people know:

- what they have to do;
- when they have to do it by;
- what other constraints they have to work to;
- what financial and other resources they can use to meet their responsibilities.

An important part of the detailed planning process is the definition of protocols. This will normally be done by whatever medical staff are involved and means laying down the procedures under which staff, for example screening nurses, will operate. If, for example, health screening involves checking the individual's blood pressure, the protocol will identify how the testing is to be done, what the 'acceptable' levels are and at what point the person's own GP will be advised of the result.

Equally, for fitness testing, the protocol will identify not only how the test is done (to ensure the safety of the individual and the validity and consistency of the results) but also existing medical conditions which would make the test inadvisable. Consistency is important from both the individual and the organisational point of view. At the individual level, two people with the same blood pressure should clearly be dealt with in the same way – all other things being equal. Consistency is also important where a long-term analysis is being done by the organisation. This analysis will be worthless if it is based on data which have not been systematically and consistently gathered.

3. ENDORSEMENT – GETTING COMMITMENT

This is really part of the assessment and planning phases, but it is so important that we have separated it off as a stage in its own right. To achieve change in an organisation, people must be persuaded to support it, and much has been written about how to do this and about how long it can be expected to take.

Exactly whose support is needed will vary from organisation to organisation, depending on, for example, whether the workforce is unionised, and other aspects of 'culture'. However, three key groups stand out in the context of supporting a healthcare programme: senior managers, those who will have to implement the programme, and those for whom the programme is being provided.

Senior management's commitment and support is vital not only because it is they who hold the purse-strings! It is ultimately senior managers who shape an organisation's culture and values, and since a healthcare programme is an expression of those values, senior management support is essential.

Another key factor is that, as was discussed in the last chapter, it is unusual to be able to make a straight financial case for improved healthcare. Other elements – such as a long-term concern for people's well-being – are likely to come into play. Also, improved healthcare is not an area for a short-term or an experimental approach. Employees who see health screening introduced will expect it to be maintained, for example, and the full benefit of certain health education campaigns may only be felt after years rather than months. For all these reasons, senior management support is essential, and this again implies that the project must be properly thought out and planned, and its sponsors in a position to 'sell the benefits' with confidence.

The healthcare programme must also be supported by those who will have to implement it – that is, the organisation's doctor(s), nurse(s) and managers. This may seem a technicality since it is likely that some of the impetus for improved healthcare provision will have come from them anyway. But this will not always be the case, and it is essential to stress that people who do not believe in the value of what they are doing are unlikely to do it very well. It may well be that this highlights some flaw in what is proposed, in which case, far better to deal with it at this stage than waste resources in implementing it unsuccessfully and then have people say 'I told you it wouldn't work' or more seriously 'I knew they weren't serious about caring for our health.'

Finally, there must be support from those for whom the healthcare programme is to be provided. All healthcare programmes require participation to be successful. You cannot force people to be screened. You can have the best 'How to stop smoking' presentation in the world, but it cannot be successful unless people come to it. Exercise equipment is just an expensive and rapidly depreciating lump of metal unless people use it. This support is not going to be forthcoming without proper consultation and communication about what is proposed.

4. TRAINING

This is really part of the next heading 'Implementation', but as with the last topic, it is so important in its own right that it needs to be dealt with separately. The implementation of a healthcare programme will often involve staff doing new things and acquiring new skills, and training needs should have been identified as part of the assessment and planning phases referred to above. Examples include:

- a nurse who is going to be running a new health education programme may need specific training in how to co-ordinate such a project. He or she may also need skills training – e.g. presentation skills;
- anyone using new equipment will need to know how to use it safely and reliably. For example, we have mentioned several times in this book the exciting possibilities offered by the desk-top blood analysers which are now available. These have the huge advantage over traditional wet chemistry methods that the analysis can be done on the spot, and the results and any necessary counselling given to the individual there and then. However, there are two essential factors if reliable results are to be obtained: the operator must be properly trained and follow a consistent

technique, and a scrupulous calibration and quality control procedure must be adopted;

- as already mentioned, much new software is available, specifically designed for applications such as COSHH record keeping, recording of hazardous substances, health screening and fitness testing. People who are going to use this software (which normally runs on a Personal Computer) will need training not only in the software itself, but also in the fundamentals of PC operation – e.g. how to switch on/off, data protection procedures, disk management, basic trouble-shooting and so on.

5. IMPLEMENTATION

This speaks for itself. It involves actually setting up and providing the healthcare facilities/services which have been agreed.

6. MONITORING

A vital stage. The planning phase should have identified how the implementation is to be monitored, with particular reference to achieving the agreed objectives. When monitoring a healthcare programme, the most important questions are:

- are the overall objectives being met?
- are there any problems – are changes necessary?
- is there anything we could do better – are changes necessary?
- what is the take-up rate (i.e. are people using whatever is being provided)?
- has what is being done been properly communicated?
- are the resource requirements in line with budget?

It is also important that this monitoring takes place at all levels of the programme. It is just as important to ask 'is there anything we could do better' at the end of each day's screening as it is to ask the same question when taking an overview of the whole programme at the end of the first year.

One of the main functions of monitoring is for the organisation to be happy that it is actually getting what it thought it was to get. But it is also important that the results are fed back into the overall management of the programme, so that the approach is one of continual improvement.

Clearly, the objective is to 'get it right first time', but this is hard in practice, especially when doing something that has never been done before, or in an area like health education where some creativity and willingness to try new ideas is needed. But by monitoring, we make sure that all the results – the successes and the failures – are fed back into the planning and management process. It is also vital to revisit the assessment phase from time to time – because needs change, and new information may come to light which would necessitate a change of focus.

Visions of the future

Good management involves making calculated judgements about the way things are likely to go in the future, and setting up an effective healthcare campaign requires not only a strategic approach but also a degree of courage. As in other areas of investment, the greatest benefit is only likely to be achieved where a long-term view is taken.

In this book, we have highlighted some of the most important trends, and in particular, the widening scope of healthcare so that it includes not only the traditional workplace hazards (although new ones keep emerging!) but also the fundamental causes of illness and premature death – such as lung cancer and coronary heart disease. There is little doubt that the trends which are now established will continue in the future, and that we will see organisations of all types and sizes doing more by way of positive planning for the healthcare of their employees.

┌─ *CHECKLIST* ─────────────────────────────────────

- Do we have a clear vision of the sort of healthcare we would like to provide, and of the benefits we would like to see coming from it?
- Are the same disciplines of planning and project management applied to healthcare as they are to other operational areas?
- Are clear objectives defined, and do arrangements exist to monitor the extent to which they are achieved in practice?
- In embarking on improved healthcare for all employees, have we done all that is possible to secure the commitment of senior managers – and the support of those who will be delivering and benefiting from the programme?
- Have we looked at the possibility of a 'healthcare audit' as a means of assessing the services currently provided?
- Does the planning process for improved healthcare include realistic budgeting and the careful identification of training needs?
- Are results assessed and the lessons learned fed back so that the overall programme is constantly being refined and improved?
- Have we communicated to all employees what we are seeking to achieve?
- Does our healthcare address the real needs of our organisation?

───

Appendix 1

Useful addresses

Action on Smoking and Health
(ASH)
5–11 Mortimer Street
London W1N 7RH
071-637-9843

Alcohol Concern
305 Grays Inn Road
London WC1X 9QF
071-833-3471

Alcoholics Anonymous
(General Office UK)
PO Box 514
11 Redcliffe Gardens
London SW10 9BG
071-352-3001

AMI Healthcare
4 Cornwall Terrace
London NW1 4QP
071-486-1266

BBC Training Videos
Woodlands
80 Wood Lane
London W12 0TT
081-576-2361

British Diabetic Association
10 Queen Anne Street
London W1M 0BD
071-323-1531

British Heart Foundation
14 Fitzhardinge Street
London W1H 4DH
071-935-0185

British Lung Foundation
12a Onslow Gardens
London SW7
071-581-0226

British Medical Association
BMA House
Tavistock Square
London WC1H 9JP
071-387-4499

British Occupational Hygiene
Society
Suite 2
Georgian House
Great Northern Road
Derby DE1 1LT
0332-298101

British Red Cross
9 Grosvenor Crescent
London SW1X 7EJ
071-235-5454

BUPA
The Provident House
24–27 Essex Street
London WC2R 3AX
071-353-5212

Cancer Research Campaign
2 Carlton House Terrace
London SW1Y 5AR
071-930-8972

Centre for Health Economics
University of York
Heslington
York YO1 5DD
0904-430000

Chest, Heart & Stroke Association
CHSA House
Whitecross Street
London EC1Y 8JJ
071-490-7999

Coronary Prevention Group
102 Gloucester Place
London W1H 3DA
071-935-2889

Family Heart Association
9 West Way
Botley
Oxford OX2 0JB
0865-798969

GKN Occupational Health
Washford House
Claybrook Drive
Washford Industrial Estate
Redditch
Worcestershire B98 0DR
0527-517747

Health Care Management Limited
Winterton House
Nixey Close
Slough
Berkshire SL1 1NG
0753-512500

Health Education Authority (HEA)
Hamilton House
Mabledon Place
London WC1H 9TX
071-383-3833

Health & Safety Executive
Baynards House
1 Chepstow Place
Westbourne Grove
London W2 4TF
071-229-3456
071-243-6000
(see telephone directory for local offices)

Health Promotion Research Trust
49–53 Regent Street
Cambridge
CB2 1AB
0223-69636

HMSO
PO Box 276
London SW8 5DT
071-873-9090

Hotel and Catering Training
Company
International House
High Street
Ealing
London W5 5DB
081-579-2400

Industrial Society
Peter Runge House
3 Carlton House Terrace
London SW1Y 5DG
071-839-4300

Institute of Alcohol Studies
Alliance House
12 Caxton Street
London SW1H OQS
071-222-5880
071-222-4001

Institute of Occupational Health
University of Birmingham
University Road West
PO Box 363
Birmingham B15 2TT
021-414-6030

Institute of Occupational Hygienists
Suite 2
Georgian House
Great Northern Road
Derby DE1 1LT
0332-298101

Institute of Occupational Medicine
8 Roxburgh Place
Edinburgh
EH8 9SU
031-667-5131

Institution of Occupational Safety &
Health
222 Uppingham Road
Leicester LE5 0QG
0533-768424
0533-763881

Institute of Personnel Management
IPM House
Camp Road
London SW19 4UX
081-946-9100

Local Health Authorities
(See telephone directory)

Medisure Marketing & Management
17 Portland Square
Bristol BS2 8SJ
0272-429331

Minerva Health Management
Limited
283 High Street
Berkhamsted
Hertfordshire HP4 1AJ
0442-870011

National Back Pain Association
31 Park Road
Teddington
Middlesex TW11 0AB
081-977-5474

National Rubella Council
311 Gray's Inn Road
London WC1X 8PT
071-837-0623

Noise Abatement Society
PO Box 8
Bromley
Kent BR2 0UH
081-460-3146

PPP
PPP House
Phillips House
Crescent Road
Tunbridge Wells
Kent TN1 2PL
0892-512345

Royal College of Nursing
20 Cavendish Square
London W1M 0AB
071-409-3333

Royal Society for the Prevention of
Accidents
Cannon House
The Priory Queensway
Birmingham
B4 6BS
021-200-2461

Royal Society of Medicine
1 Wimpole Street
London W1M 8AE
071-408-2119

Royal College of Physicians
11 St Andrew's Place
Regent's Park
London NW1 4LE
071-935-1174

St John Ambulance
1 Grosvenor Crescent
London SW1X 7EF
071-235-5231

Scottish Health Education Group
Woodburn House
Canaan Lane
Edinburgh
EH10 4SG
031-447-8044

Scriptographic Publications
Channing House
Butts Road
Alton
Hampshire GU34 1ND
0420-541738

Society of Occupational Medicine
6 St Andrew's Place
Regent's Park
London NW1 4LB
071-486-2641

Sports Council
16 Upper Woburn Place
London WC1H 0QP
071-388-1277

Terrence Higgins Trust
52–54 Gray's Inn Road
London WC1X 8JU
071-831-0330

Appendix 2

Bibliography

Smoking Policies at Work
Health Education Authority

Smoking Policy Manual
ASH

Can You Avoid Cancer?
Health Education Authority, 1989

Why Exercise?
David Ashton & Bruce Davies, Basil Blackwell Limited, 1986

Health & Safety Beyond the Workplace
Edited by Lester V. Cralley, Lewis J. Cralley and W. Clark Cooper, John Wiley & Sons, Inc., 1990

The Complete Guide to Stress Management
Dr Chandra Patel, Macdonald Optima, 1989

Living With Stress
Cary L. Cooper, Rachel D. Cooper and Lynn H. Eaker, Penguin Books Limited, 1988

Think Well Feel Great
Donald Norfolk, Michael Joseph Limited, 1990

Work and Health
Andrew Melhuish, Penguin Books Limited, 1982

Health Promotion in Primary Health Care – An Introduction
English National Board, 1989

The Picture of Health
Dumfries and Galloway Health and Lifestyle Survey, 1990

A Guide to European Community Legislation on Health and Safety at Work
Michael Murray, Association of the British Pharmaceutical Industry, 1990

Coronary Heart Disease: Reducing the Risk – a reader
Wiley Medical in association with the Open University, 1987

Dangerous Chemicals – Emergency First Aid Guide
Croner Publications

So You Want to Stop Smoking
Health Education Authority

Passive Smoking – A Health Hazard
Imperial Cancer Research Fund, 1991

The Corporate Healthcare Revolution
David Ashton, Kogan Page Limited, 1989

AIDS and First Aid
CBI

Managing For Attendance
CBI

Promoting Health – A Practical Guide
Ewles and Simnett, John Wiley & Sons, 1985

Living with Risk
The British Medical Association, Penguin Books, 1990

Screening in Health Care
Walter W. Holland and Susie Stewart, Nuffield Provincial Hospitals Trust, 1990

Getting in Shape
Gay Search and David Denison, New English Library, 1988

The Medical Risks of Life
Stephen Lock and Tony Smith, Penguin Books Limited, 1976

The State of the Public Health for the Year 1989
HMSO

The Nation's Health – A Strategy for the 1990's
Edited by Alwyn Smith and Bobbie Jacobson, King Edward's Hospital Fund for London

Index

cresol splashes, treatment for 71
crime 118, 121
culture, company 97–8
cuts *see* accidents
cyanide 71
cycling 151, 158, 164

dance 159
darts 163
death, premature 1, 8–9, 84, 198, 200, 210
  main causes of 47–52
  reduction in 190, 191–2, 194
delegation 115
demonstrations 180–2
dentistry 86–7
Department of Health 119, 137, 200
depression 106, 152
dermatitis 5, 27, 89, 200
design/designers 6, 21
DHSS 53
diabetes 53, 60–61, 86, 158, 169
Dickens, Charles 2
diet 14, 81, 86, 168, 178, 182, 199
disaster planning *see* emergency plans
divorce 118
dizziness 158
doctors 6, 27, 62, 75, 84–5, 188, 201, 207, 208
dose-response relationship 10–12
drinking *see* alcohol
driving as additional stress factor 97, 106–7
driving, defensive 94–5, 171
  drunken 121–2
  safe 46, 87, 94–5
drug abuse 61, 146
drug tests 61
Dumfries and Galloway Health Board exercise survey 162–3
dust 5, 21, 91, 172
  extraction 7, 188
  samplers 188

ear protection zones 32, 33
eating habits, change in 99, 200
EC Directives 12, 18, 20, 38–40, 200
EC Directive 86/188/EC (Protection

of Workers from the Risks Related to Exposure to Noise at Work) 31, 40
EC Directive on Manual Handling 34
EC programme on safety, hygiene and health at work 39–40
ECG (electrocardiogram) 56
education *see* training
electrocution 94
electrolytic chromium process 27
emergency plans 23, 29, 66, 77–8
emphysema 141, 171
Employee Assistance Programme (EAPs) 16, 88, 115
Employers' Liability Insurance 73
Employment Medical Advisor (EMA) 27
employment package enhanced by healthcare 14, 153, 198
engineers 6
environmental improvements 63, 91–2, 112, 141, 199
epidemiology 5
ergonomics/ergonomists 6, 39, 92–4, 112, 114
Ewles and Simnett 178, 179
executive medicals and health screening 14–15, 47
exercise 88, 150–66, 168, 194, 200
  aerobic/anaerobic 158, 164
  benefits and importance of 80, 110–11, 150–53
  bikes 188, 208
  facilities at work 162–5, 205, 208
  lack of 53
  risks of 154, 174
  programmes in Japanese companies 153
eye injuries from sport 154
eye irritation 140
eyesight 46
  testing 51, 87, 192

Factories Act 1961 2, 3
Factory Acts 2, 4
Faculty of Occupational Medicine 90
falls 94

false negative and false positive
  results 56–7, 60
family history 53, 169, 173
family life, disruption of 107–8
  pressures of 107
farming 68
films/videos/slides 179–80, 181
fire procedure 77
fires 94, 141
first aid 7, 15, 66, 94, 194
  equipment 69–71
  room 70–71
  see also Health and Safety (First
    Aid) Regulations 1981: Health
    and Safety at Work Act 1974
first aiders ('suitable persons') 67–9,
  73–4
  danger of contracting AIDS 74
  personal liability of 73–4
fishing 163
fitness 47, 150–66, 199
  measuring 155–7
  testing 58–9, 150, 192, 207, 209
food handling 46, 199
food poisoning 43, 77
Forced Expired Volume (FEV) 157
Forced Vital Capacity (FVC) 157
Ford, company smoking policy 139
Forrest Report 53
Framingham, Mass., CHD study of
  54, 169
Friedman and Rosenman 103
fumes 91, 92, 113

gamma-glutamyltransferase, test for
  132
gas detectors 188
Gas Transfer Test 157
give-aways 181
GKN Occupational Health 183
glaucoma 87
Glazer, Dr Howard 103–5
Glazer Stress Control Lifestyle
  Questionnaire 104–5
golf 159
gout 61
guarding of machinery 2, 5

Haggard, Dr Spencer 140

Harvard University graduates, fitness
  study of 151
Hawthorne Effect 192
hazardous conditions, substituting
  safe conditions for 91
hazardous substances, control of 23,
  89, 209
  see also COSHH Regulations 1988
hazardous substances, definition of
  21–3
  EC symbols for 22
  maintenance of 23
  storage and disposal of 26
headaches 106
Health and Morals of Apprentices
  Act 1802 2
Health and Safety at Work Act
  1979 4, 7, 12, 18–40, 60
Health and Safety Commission
  (HSC) 34, 35
Health and Safety (Enforcing
  Authority) Regulations 1989
  35
Health and Safety Executive 18, 21,
  27, 30, 46, 66, 90, 133
  Employment Nursing Advisory
    Service 74
  publications 121
Health and Safety (First Aid)
  Regulations 1981 66–7, 69, 75
Health and Safety Information for
  Employees Regulations 1989 36
healthcare programmes 1, 13, 14,
  16, 62, 75, 83–4, 93, 121
  benefits of 189–96
  costs of 186–9
  management of 198–9, 201–10
  monitoring of 209–10
  planning of 198, 204–207
Healthcare Management 76–7
health, occupational *see* occupational
  health
health clubs 16
health education 15, 43, 51, 61,
  62, 63, 118, 167–84
  employer's role in 83–4, 130–31,
  176–83, 209–10
  materials 183
  planning effective campaigns
  176–84

Health Education Authority 131,
133, 140, 178, 183
publications 142, 148
Health Education Council 163–4
health farms 199
health, general, as important as
occupational health 13, 83
health hazards 5–6 and throughout
health, importance of in workplace
3
vs. safety 8–9, 81–3
health issues, general awareness of
20, 198
health, occupational *see* occupational
health
health screening 14–15, 42–65, 85,
132, 150, 182, 187, 193, 209
frequency of 64
guidelines 44–6
introduction of 63–4, 204
on-site/off-site 63–4
pre-employment 85, 188
providers 62–3
healthy eating *see* diet
hearing aids 10
hearing tests 59
hearing loss, noise induced 6, 9–12,
174, 183, 194, 200
heart attack 56, 74–5, 138
exercise after 152
heart rate 59, 99, 156
heart disease *see* coronary heart
disease (CHD)
heating 112, 199
hepatitis 74
alcoholic 122
Hippocrates 4
HIV 61, 74
HMSO publications 69
Holland and Stewart 44, 45
Homes and Rahe stress scale 101–2
hospitals, proximity of 69, 71
Hougham, John 139
housework 162
human performance curve 100
hydrogen fluoride (HF)/hydrofluoric
acid 71
hygiene 84
hygienists, occupational *see*
occupational hygienists

hypertension 60, 86, 154
hypnotism 148

illness 1, 8–9, 10, 12, 37, 38, 43,
82, 84, 93, 117–8, 189, 190,
193, 194, 195, 198, 210
at work 66–7, 75, 77–8
stress-related 101–3
Imperial Cancer Research Fund 140
Improvement Notices 35, 36
Industrial Tribunal 36
inefficiency 84
see also productivity, reduced
infections 81
information *see* health education;
training/trainers
injury at work 8, 36, 66–7, 75, 81,
93
inspectors *see* HSE: Local
Authorities
Institute of Occupational Safety and
Health 82
Institution of Safety and Health 92
Ionising Radiation Regulations 1985
21
ionising radiation 18
irritability 99
irritant substance 21, 28, 89

James I of England 136
jaundice 61, 122
jogging 151, 159–60
Johnson and Johnson 'Live for Life'
programme 193, 201
joint pains 158
judo 160

kidney disease 55, 60, 61
kidney failure 122
Knebel, Fletcher 145
Korsakoff's syndrome 123

laughter 110
lawyers 6
lead 18, 20, 23
see also Control of Lead at Work
Regulations 1980
Legionnaire's disease 19, 89, 200
leg vessel disease 55

posters 167, 178
  see also publicity
posture 92, 155
postural injury 89
pregnancy 92, 124, 136, 200
presentation skills 208
preventive dentistry 86–7
preventive healthcare 28, 75, 77, 81
preventive health screening 84–5
pride in work 97
private medical insurance 76
Private Patients' Plan (PPP) 76
productivity, raised 185, 190, 192
productivity, reduced 126, 133, 192
professional services 80–95
  see also ergonomists: occupational
  hygienists: occupational
  psychologists: physiotherapists
profit making 16, 185–97
Prohibition Notices 35, 36
protective clothing 26, 92
  see also personal protective
  equipment (PPE)
protein 61
protestant work ethic 110
publicity 63, 167, 189
pulse rate 156

Quality Circles 107
QUALY (Quality Adjusted Life
  Year) 191–2
questionnaires, use of 143, 177,
  181
quizzes 181

radiation 81, 89, 91
  see also ionising radiation
Ramazzini, Bernardino 4
records/data 26, 27, 29, 71, 84, 93,
  209
Red Cross 69, 74
Registered Safety Practitioners 93
relaxation 81, 88, 108, 109, 111–2
repetitive strain injury 89, 200
respiratory diseases 48, 49, 51, 52,
  55, 84, 140, 141, 168, 171–2,
  191
Respiratory Protective Equipment
  (RPE) 26, 30, 92

risk factors in disease 42, 53–5, 84,
  170
risk, minimising 28, 31–2, 90–1
road accidents *see* motor accidents
Robens, Lord Alfred 3
Robens Report 1972 3
rowing machines 188
Royal College of Physicians 137,
  140
Royal College of Psychiatrists 125
rugby 154
running 152, 154, 159–60, 164

'Safety and Health Practitioner,
  The' 82
safety at work 2–3, 19, 29, 39,
  92–4
safety professionals 92–4 *and
  throughout*
Safety Representatives and Safety
  Committee Regulations 1978
  7–8
safety signs 22, 33, 40
St Johns Ambulance 69, 75
Scottish Health Education Board
  131
screening *see* health screening
self-employment, health and safety
  in 19
sewage workers 4
sex (male) as risk factor 53, 169
sex distribution in workforce 46
Shaftesbury, Earl of 2
shift system 107
shipbuilding 9
shock therapy 148
sick building syndrome 89,
  199–200
silicosis 172
Single European Market *see* EC
  Directives
skiing 154
skin problems 88
sleeping pattern, change in 99
smokers, support for 144
smoking, cigarette 5, 51, 52, 53,
  55, 81, 84, 136, 151, 167, 169,
  171, 172, 173, 180, 181, 193,
  199, 200
smoking, passive 136, 139–41, 176

smoking, stopping 145–8, 168, 170, 173, 208
smoking policies 139, 140–8
  smokers' reactions to 141–2
snooker 160, 163
Society of Occupational Medicine 7
solvents 23, 28, 91
spillage *see* emergency plans
sphygmomanometers 188
spirometry 52, 157
sport 150–62
Sports Council 163–4
squash 156, 160
stamina 154–5, 158–62, 164
Standing Medical Advisory Committee 191
Statutory Sick Pay (SSP) 195
stomach disorders 88
stress 14, 53, 54, 88, 97–116, 146, 150, 153, 169, 193, 197
  and levels of responsibility 106–8
  awareness of 108–9
  in the work place 105–8
  management 81, 88, 97, 109–115
  mental effects of 109
  physical effects of 98–100, 108–9
  positive and negative 101
  tests 59–60
stress-induced drinking 127
strength 154–5, 158–62
stroke *see* cerebrovascular disease
suffocation 94
suicide 49
  attempted 118
suppleness 154–5, 158–62
swimming 151, 154, 160

team games 161
tennis 160–61
Third Party Administrator (TPA) 76–7
time at work, loss of 63–4, 86–7, 93, 132, 189
time management 112–3
tinnitus 10

tooth decay 86
total lung capacity (TLC) 157
toxic substances 21, 28, 36, 46
trade unions 7, 20, 42, 90, 134
training/trainers 6, 13, 18, 29, 32, 51, 62, 68, 94–5, 130, 192, 194–5, 203, 207, 208–9
  see also health education
1,1,1-trichloroethane 23
triglycerides, test for 56
tuberculosis 52
TUC 12
  see also trade unions
typewriter correction fluid, thinner for 23

UK General Household Survey on exercise 163
UK Independent Scientific Committee on Smoking and Health 140
ulcers 88
urine tests 60–61

ventilation 2, 92, 97, 199
vibration 81, 89, 91
vinyl chloride monomer 7, 27
violence 117, 121
visual display units (VDUs) 9, 19, 34–5, 59, 87, 92, 199, 200

walking 161, 162, 163
washing solutions 71
wastes 28
weight 86
  loss 47
  training 161–2, 164
well woman screening 57
Wernicke's encephalopathy 123
'white finger' 89
Wilson and Jungner 44
workload pressure 97, 113
World Health Organisation 44

yoga 162